Bishop Schnase,

Growing a church
is a choice!

CONNECT

HOW TO GROW YOUR CHURCH IN 28 DAYS GUARANTEED

DON CORDER

WHAT READERS ARE SAYING

"Years ago I was pastoring a little church in a little town with a handful of people. The church was broke and I was ready to give up. Don Corder sat me down, and said, 'Growing a church is simple. It's just not easy.' On his back porch, he wrote down the things I needed to do. One at a time, I started doing those things. My church began to grow. Today our ministry is in multiple sites in multiple towns, serving thousands. *Connect* is that very plan written on that porch all those years ago. I wish I had had this book when I was starting out. Things would have been a lot easier.

Matt Young

Senior Pastor

LifeChurch

Southwest, Ohio

"We are living in a global conflagration of spiritual warfare; and the devastation isn't somewhere else, *it's in our own pews*. Everyone knows something is happening. The real issue is to identify the problem and then produce a genuine solution. "

Paul Louis Cole

President of Christian Men's Network Worldwide

Founding pastor of C3 Church in Dallas

Dallas, TX

"I have used the strategy in *Connect* in two churches and both churches saw increased professions of faith, community engagement, and giving, as well as new members. If you are looking for something that will jump-start kingdom growth in your church, I highly recommend reading this book."

Joe Fox
Senior Pastor
Grace United Methodist Church
Washington Courthouse, Ohio

"No one I've ever met combines profound operational acumen, authentic spirituality, vast experience, and engaging communication style like Don Corder does. Truth be told—no one comes close. You wouldn't have picked up this book if you weren't serious about the Great Commission, passionate about the local church as the center of God's plan and determined that your church be a bastion of health and growth. I know that the twenty-eight tasks outlined in *Connect* will work *because they are working*, right now, in churches large and small, old and new, all across the country. The only thing you've got to lose are empty seats."

Rick Nash
COO
The Kairos Company
Glendale, California

"A few years ago, I asked Don Corder for some advice on growing my church. He shared a whole new way of looking at the way a church grows by focusing on how people form relationships in the twenty-first century. "Going" starts with an act of faith and "making disciples" starts as a spiritual quest, but *connecting* the church with people *starts with intentionality.* Four years later, our church attendance has doubled."

Michael Phillips
Senior Pastor
Kingdom Life Church
Baltimore, Maryland

"This stuff works! My church has been working with Don since 2013 and have seen significant growth. *Connect* shares his wisdom and experience from decades of helping churches grow all over the country. If you've been struggling, the struggle is over. Buy this book and do what it says. You'll be glad you did."

Jon Ferguson
Senior Pastor
Stillwater United Methodist Church
Dayton, Ohio

"Don Corder understands the challenges organizations face in the twenty-first century. More importantly, Don has a heart for God, His people, and the people His people need to reach to grow His kingdom. This book spells out, in an engaging and conversational style, a proven approach to fulfill the Great Commission in a culture that doesn't consider a relationship with God essential. He'll help you think realistically about the task your church faces and give you proven strategies so your congregation can thrive."

Reverend Mark Youngkin
Professor of Communication and Leadership
Valor Christian College
Columbus, Ohio

"Don Corder is a gifted communicator, and he shares his gift with all of us in *Connect!* In it, you will look through the eyes of a master and learn how to connect your church with the people who live around you. Apply the practical action steps described in this book, and your church will grow."

Ronnie Harrison
Senior Pastor
Kingdom Center Church
Louisville, Kentucky

"The first time Don Corder showed me the ideas written in his new book, *Connect*. I thought to myself, "That will preach!" It is our job to first connect people with the church and then connect people with each other, all while teaching and serving. This is how disciples have been made for 2,000 years. This book changed the way I look at church communications."

Dr. Jody Ray
Senior Pastor
Mt. Bethel Church
Marietta, GA

"*Buy this book!* Execute the twenty-eight action items. Grow your church. A must read for everyone in ministry."

Shannon Lee
Executive Director
Relā
Dublin, OH

"I've known Don Corder for nearly fifteen years. He is an industry thought leader when it comes to church administration and growth. Don is as practical as he is brilliant. In *Connect*, you will find a turnkey plan guaranteed to grow your church, *but you have to execute the plan*. No one ever grew a ministry by waiting and hoping. Get this book. Do what it says."

Jon Laria
CFO
OneHope
Pompano Beach, Florida

"Don Corder is a hidden gem in the kingdom. He has a passion for the Great Commission, the church, and for pastors. I have never met a person more dedicated to growing the local church. This book is a gift. Execute the steps and your church will grow."

Brad White
Executive Director
IAK Donors
Washington, D.C.

"Surveys on religion in America have revealed that fewer people than ever before claim a Christian affiliation. We must realize that the way in which people form relationships, especially with institutions, is different than it once was. This day and age calls for the church to be more intentional and proactive than ever before. Don Corder presents twenty-eight practical steps that *will help any church* to *grow*. I had the privilege of serving as Don's pastor some years ago, and I know his heart for reaching people with the gospel. I am looking forward to implementing the steps outlined in *Connect* in the church where I currently serve."

Dr. Ken Alford
Senior Pastor,
Crossroads Baptist Church,
Valdosta, Georgia

CONNECT

How to Grow Your Church in **28** Days - Guaranteed

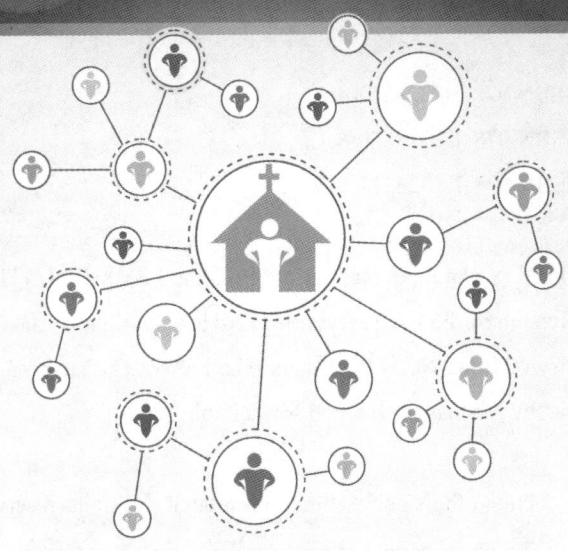

DON CORDER

HigherLife Development Services, Inc.

PO Box 623307

Oviedo, Florida 32762

(407) 563-4806

www.ahigherlife.com

Printed in the United States of America

10 9 8 7 6 5 4 3 2 1

Library of Congress Cataloging-in-Publication Data

Paperback book: ISBN 978-1-7326377-4-0
Hardback book: ISBN 978-1-7328859-8-1
eBook: ISBN 978-1-7326377-5-7

The Great Commission

Go therefore and make disciples of all nations, baptizing them in the name of the Father and of the Son and of the Holy Spirit, teaching them to observe all that I have commanded you.

And behold, I am with you always, to the end of the age

(Matthew 28:19-20).

TABLE OF CONTENTS

A NOTE FROM THE AUTHOR

When I set out to write this book many of my friends and mentors encouraged me not to write it. I lead a nonprofit organization that virtually manages church communication and growth and they said giving away what we sell is not good business. Some people reminded me that I have a responsibility to my employees who earn their livings and support their families growing churches for our clients. Most of the people who work at The Provisum Group (including me) walked away from prosperous careers in the private sector to serve the kingdom of God by taking their incredible skills and vast experience and dedicating their lives to growing churches. Giving churches our hard-earned, proven and tested church growth strategies in the form of this book just seems counterintuitive.

But serving God and His kingdom is not always easy. It doesn't always make sense. Sometimes it is scary. Most of the time it takes faith. So I chose to lean into the truth that God is good, He is who He says He is, and His Word is true. Twenty years ago when I walked away from industry to serve the church, I decided to trust God for my daily bread and do everything in my power to grow His kingdom on earth.

The book you hold in your hands contains one possible future for your church. In it you will find twenty-eight different once-a-day tasks. If you will do one every day and keep doing them, your church will grow. This book is the exact strategy we execute every day for our church clients all over the country. Our church growth strategy is a culmination of decades of trial and error. If something worked well, we kept doing it. If something didn't work, we figured out why and did our best to fix it. If it still didn't work, we stopped doing it. We are not guessing and hoping here. This strategy works. But you have to be faithful and follow the plan.

My prayer for you and this book is that you find at least one thing on its pages that makes your life in ministry a little easier and grows your church, because when your church grows, somebody meets Jesus and this world and the world to come is a better place. Blessings!

- Don Corder

FOREWORD: THE AUDIENCE

If you want to grow your church, you have to connect people who live far from Jesus with people who live for Jesus. You have to connect people. This is not a secret. This is not new. But how we connect the church with the neighborhood and community around us has changed dramatically over the last forty years.

In this book, we're going to talk about the groups of people in your church and in your community a little differently. We'll break them down into five groups throughout the rest of the book: the saints, the disciples, the undiscipled, the community, and the neighborhood.

- The "saints" are the people who have accepted for themselves the responsibility of making people into disciples. The saints are the children's leaders, pastors, elders, deacons, and Bible study leaders, the ones who understand the Bible and do most of the disciple-making in your ministry.

- The "disciples" are the people who joined your community of faith, made a decision for Christ, and proactively seek to grow in their faith. They bring their children to Sunday school, live generously, attend the studies of Scripture, do the work of the church, and serve others in mission.

- The "undiscipled" are people who may or may not identify as a Christian, but did not grow up in a church. Undiscipled people do not have an experiential context or learned precept for Christian living. They have yet to accept the personal responsibility of their own discipleship. Undiscipled people are the raw material of disciple making.

- The "community" is anyone whose contact information you possess. You might not know their names, but you have at least their e-mail addresses or cell phone numbers on record.

- The "neighborhood" are those people who live around your church, but for whom you have no connection whatsoever and possess no contact information.

This book will walk you through a process of connecting with the neighborhood and community around your church and then integrating them into the disciple-making process of your ministry. Understanding how these different groups make connection decisions and connect with people and institutions is an important and often neglected component of growing a church in the twenty-first century.

INTRODUCTION: THE THEOLOGY FOR GROWTH

Since the day Jesus ascended to heaven, Christians have been commissioned to go into all the world and make disciples of all people. This apostolic mission is one of the most important faith tenets that distinguishes Christianity from all other religions.

> *Go therefore and make disciples of all nations, baptizing*
> *them in the name of the Father and of the Son and of the Holy*
> *Spirit, teaching them to observe all that I have commanded*
> *you. And behold, I am with you always, to the end of the age*
> *(Matthew 28:19-20).*

What happens between "go" and "make"? There has to be something. The Bible does not say it, but we can reasonably assume it's up to us to fill in the white space between the lines of this Scripture to fulfill the Great Commission for our generation. It is reasonable for us to infer that between "go" and "make" is exactly what Jesus and the disciples did in their day, which is, connect. The church can't reach all people if we don't go; and we cannot make disciples if we do not connect with people. This mission has not changed. However, the world has changed and so has the way we go and connect.

In the first few hundred years of ministry, the church in the West was a minority religious sect in a majority secular culture. Somewhere between Emperor Theodosius I making Christianity the "religion of the empire" in the fourth century AD and Emperor Charlemagne reviving "the Holy Roman Empire" in the early ninth century, the church became a leading force in a majority Christian culture. The church remained more or less in this leading role until the late twentieth century, but I don't think anyone would argue that today, the church in the West is once again a minority religious sect in a majority secular culture.

In the first few centuries of the church, the order of ministry for a minority religious sect in a majority secular culture was:

- Connect

- Evangelize

- Convert

- Disciple

"Going" meant actually traveling to a new place where most people knew little to nothing about Jesus and His kingdom. Once in this new place, the missionary/disciple would become part of the community and connect with his neighbor or her coworker. Relationships would form and grow until the credibility of the disciple was established in the eyes of the non-believer. Then the disciple would share the good news with his new friends. This led to the culminating moment of conversion when the non-believer became a new creation in Christ and then the process of training disciples or disciple-making began.

As a leading force in a majority Christian culture the order of ministry changed. The order of ministry became:

- Evangelize

- Convert

- Connect

- Disciple

Through most of the Dark Ages, it was hard to tell where the state ended and the church began. In many cases, the king of the domain was also the head of the church. As such, "going" was funded by the king and conversion was mandated by the state. There was little need to "connect" or "disciple." By the mid-twentieth century, there were few places left in Western civilization in which there was no church and no one had heard of Jesus. We were rapidly running out of places to go. By the late twentieth century, "going" and "making" was being sadly replaced by "hoping" and "waiting."

Let me illustrate. Fifty years ago in the West, if someone walked through the door of a church for the first time, he was probably looking for "a church," meaning they just moved to the area and needed a new place of worship or for some reason decided to look for a new place to worship. Today, when someone visits a church, she is probably looking for "an answer." Before, almost everyone was "well-churched," meaning they had attended church for most of their lives, or at least believed they *should* be attending. They knew what was expected of them inside and outside of the church. They also knew what to expect when they began attending a new church. In order to successfully grow a church, churches just needed to meet the expectations of the new visitors. Churches focused on making worship, preaching, programming, and facilities the best they could be.

One of the most distinguishing characteristics of this late Christian-era church was the way it connected with people. Most of the connection methods were passive and rear-loaded. They were passive in that they were dependent on the new visitor initiating the connection. The church would wait for the visitor to fill out the connection card, visit the connection center, register for a new member's class, attend Sunday school, or request a meeting with the pastor. Connecting with other believers and developing relationships with them was "rear-loaded": it was a byproduct of the engagement initiated by the new visitor.

This all changed in the early twenty-first century. Who hasn't heard the name of Jesus in the United States and Europe? As of the writing of this book, if you ask 100% of Americans if they are a Christian, seventy five percent (www.news.gallup.com/poll/224642/2017-update-americans-religion. aspx) will say yes, but only twenty-one percent will be in church on Sunday. Only eight percent of Americans will attend church three or more Sundays in a month. In the post-Christian era, people are not just "un-churched"; more often than not, they are "undiscipled." Undiscipled people are the raw material of disciple-making in the twenty-first century.

Today, people visiting for the very first time are probably looking for an answer. The church can no longer assume that visitors are well-churched, know what is expected of them, know what they want, or what to expect from a church. Many times, there is some life event like an illness, financial crisis, or moral failing that precipitates a person visiting a church for the first time or for the first time in a very long time. Many times, undiscipled people walk through the doors of a church with a giant "should" in them. People who walk into a new church with a big "should" in them are looking for spirituality in everything: "I *should* solve this," "I *should* try church," "I should try something different than what I've been doing." When they walk through the doors of the church for the first time or the first time in a very long time, they expect the rafters to rattle, the ground to shake, and the angels to sing. This is their moment. "OK, God, I am here. I have done my part. Do Yours."

It is like joining a gym in January. Most people join a gym in January because they have about ten pounds of holiday "should" on them. In the same way, people are visiting a church because they think they "should" in order to find something they need. But just like the people who join a gym in January, many quit going by February.

Post-Christian era visitors do not know the routine. They don't know how to be discipled or even that it's an option: they do not know if discipling is something that could solve many of their problems or not. At best, they become passive participants in their own discipleship. What they do not know is that the disciples and saints are passively waiting for these new undiscipled visitors to proactively raise their hands and say "I am ready to connect. What do you want me to do?" The Post-Christian era visitor has very little firsthand experience with church and walks through the doors of the church with secular values and expectations.

Imagine if you are visiting a foreign country and walked into a restaurant. In this country, the culture is different. In this foreign culture, it is considered rude for the waiters in restaurants to approach diners until the diner initiates the process by standing and summoning them to the table with an obvious hand motion. But you don't share the same culture and are unaware of what is considered proper behavior for diners in this foreign culture. There were twenty staff people standing around talking. Not one makes eye contact with you or proactively reaches out to you to initiate a connection. There was a big sign out front, saying "Visitors Welcome," but no one spoke to you, helped you to a seat, or brought you a cup of water to quench your thirst. What would this make you think? How would you would feel? Would you come back?

Do you see the inherent disconnect between the late Christian era Church members and the Post-Christian era undiscipled visitor? Once again, as a minority religious sect in a majority secular culture, the order of ministry has reverted back to:

- Connect

- Evangelize

- Convert

- Disciple

Connecting with undiscipled people has to be front-loaded in a relationship, meaning *the church has to make the first move and proactively provide the energy that leads to connection with visitors and undiscipled people.* Most churches today are still acting like a leading force in a majority Christian culture and passively waiting for connection to happen as a visitor-initiated by-product of being in church. Both groups are waiting for the other to take the first step and initiate connection. It is a perfect recipe for decline and decay.

This is why I wrote *Connect*.

The church cannot "make" disciples of undiscipled people if we do not connect with them. If we are going to fulfill the Great Commission, the church is going to have to take the lead in this Post-Christian era and initiate connection with everyone we meet, and in everything we do. Technology has replaced much of the "going" of the past. The making of disciples has not changed much in 2,000 years, but the in-between — the connect part — has changed dramatically in the last forty years.

In this book, I am going to provide you with a literal checklist of twenty-eight tested and proven tasks that will improve the "connect" of your church, so you can engage in "making" disciples and fulfill your purpose, the Great Commission. If you, or a designated staff member or volunteer, does each of these tasks once a day and keeps doing them, you will connect with more undiscipled people, your church will grow, and you will receive the deep satisfaction and fulfillment of achieving your purpose.

DAY
1

CAST THE VISION

The vision of every church is the first macro — the Great Commission: to make disciples of all people everywhere. From that macro-vision, churches today more or less adopt a vision that is either attractional or missional. The attractional churches want to build crowds. The missional churches want to make disciples. But the vision is always to serve the macro — the Great Commission. To make disciples of "all nations" requires both bringing people to a place of evangelism and then making those people into disciples.

One of the things that separates Christianity from all major faiths is that we have an apostolic mission. We are the only major faith group that grows by assimilating the hearts and minds of people. No other faith group is geared to grow, or has an incumbency to grow, like ours.

This book does not address disciple-making. Disciple-making is the role of ministry. What we're teaching about is creating *an environment* and providing the *raw material* for disciple-making to occur. In *Connect*, we will assume the challenges you face are not in making disciples, but are in connecting with the undiscipled people who live all around you. We will give you a step-by-step plan that connects your church or ministry with undiscipled people and gets them to connect with the disciples and saints in your church or ministry. We will also assume that church leadership is called by God, and that God Himself has planted in you His vision for the flock you lead.

To that end, the church needs to make sure that everyone we lead understands this global disciple-making mission as well as the specific vision God has for your local body of believers. One thing I learned a long time ago is that there are many gifted speakers but far fewer gifted listeners. As such, if we are going to inject this God-given mandate to evangelize the world (at least your piece of it), we will have to be relentless in the communication of that vision.

One mistake I see many ministry leaders make is the assumption that everyone already knows. The number one rule in marketing and communica-

"THE NUMBER ONE RULE IN MARKETING AND COMMUNICATION (ESPECIALLY IN MINISTRY) IS 'YOU ARE NOT THEM.'"

tion (especially in ministry) is "You are not them." Here are three questions you could ask every person you lead in ministry:

1. What is the greatest commandment in the Bible?

2. What is the Great Commission?

3. Who was the apostle Paul and what did he do?

How many laypeople that you lead in ministry do you think could answer all three questions correctly? Give it a try. You might be surprised. Over the years, I have seen many pastors' and ministry leaders' jaws drop when they see how few people in their churches today have what just thirty years ago was considered a very basic understanding of Scripture. This lack of spiritual and scriptural understanding is a byproduct of our Post-Christian era of spiritual relativism.

If you would like to send a little survey to your congregation asking these three questions go to www.connectandgrowyourchurch.com/survey and we will set it up for you.

It is so important that everyone understands that the reason the church exists is to make disciples of Christ for the transformation of the world. As leaders in the body of Christ, it is our job to make sure everyone we lead knows this mission and embraces the vision. In addition, it is important that all the disciples and saints know the Post-Christian era order of ministry, which now is:

- Connect

- Evangelize

- Convert

- Disciple

To make sure everyone knows the reason the church exists and that they see this new order of ministry, we as leaders must ensure that this vision is discussed over and over and over again: in every service, in every class, in every small group, in every staff meeting, in every communication. We must make sure that everyone "has heard."

DAY 1 CAST THE VISION

Ask all the leaders and staff in your church these questions: What did you do this week to help people know that we are a people called to make disciples of all people for the transformation of the world? What will you do next week?

DAY
2

DEFINE YOUR BRAND

When we talk about your church's "brand," we are not talking about a logo, a slogan, or a mission statement. Your brand is what you want your saints and disciples to say to their friends and neighbors. Your brand is what you want the community and the neighborhood to say about your church.

A typical church branding statement could be: "Green Park Fellowship is committed to making fully devoted followers of Jesus Christ." That sounds like a short, crisp statement that anyone in the church could memorize, right? Now imagine one of your life group leaders looking over the fence as her neighbor is weeding a flowerbed and saying, "Hey, you need to come to our church because we're committed to making fully devoted followers of Jesus Christ!" The best response your leader would probably get is a hollow

"DEFINING YOUR BRAND IS DONE BY CREATING MESSAGING AND MOMENTS THAT CAUSE PEOPLE TO SAY THINGS BEHIND YOUR BACK THAT YOU WANT THEM TO SAY."

stare and a weak nod. That's not our desired result, is it? Undiscipled people aren't scrambling for reasons to get up on Sunday mornings and become devoted Christ followers.

Defining your brand is done by creating messaging and moments that cause people to say things behind your back that you want them to say.

One church we work with has a committee-created, church-body-approved statement that cannot be changed. It is also so lengthy and cumbersome, it cannot be used. We solved that communication problem by creating an internal branding statement that no one will ever see written. It wasn't adopted by a committee nor printed into the church by-laws. It isn't framed on a wall in the church office. The "branding" is simply this: "It's that really big church with all those nice people who do all that really cool stuff."

In communications, whether this church is loading up a truck of young people to help flood victims, or hosting a Parent's Day Out, all of their communication is weighed against this message: that big church full of nice people who do cool stuff. We've so permeated their communications with this message that now the saints and disciples tell their friends, "Come with me! You'll love all these really nice people. And they do such cool stuff." The result is that the community and neighborhood see that congregation as the big church with the nice people who take care of other people and do cool stuff.

Back in the 1990s there was a book by Steven Covey called *7 Habits of Highly Effective People*. One of the chapters was titled "Start with the End in Mind." Author Steven Covey challenged readers to decide what we want on their tombstones. He encouraged the reader to consider what they wanted their epitaph to be. I'll tell you mine:

"Here lies a man of integrity and respect. He loved his God. He loved his family. He loved his fellow man and he always tried to do his best."

Now, how am I going to get that on my tombstone? I'm going to have to live it every day of my life in front of everyone I meet.

An epitaph is something that is said when you're gone. Same with branding. What do you want the neighborhood and community to say about your church behind your back? Your branding statement, whether only used internally or emblazoned on the wall, challenges you to live up to it every day. Create the message and live the message. That's how your church is going to get the reputation (or brand) it wants.

Most churches create a committee that ends up with a wordy statement, often just to accommodate the thoughts and feelings of the people in the room tasked with coming up with the statement. The statement may please the ear, but does it connect with people? If you're a communications leader or pastor, and for some reason you're unable to change the mission or vision statements of your church, you can still write one that works for you. One church we work with started with this committee-driven statement, "We are Christ followers who care enough to share truth, show grace, and shine love to our community; and an evangelistic force, equipped and spiritually educated, to impact culture beyond the walls of the church to all people everywhere." This is a fine thing to aspire to be. There's nothing wrong with any of those words. You just can't very well say that to the neighbor over the fence. It doesn't connect.

As you work through your branding, keep your statement short. I advocate making statements no longer than a haiku poem —17 syllables. One organization we worked with had a pretty wordy branding statement that had included things they were against. What they were for and what they were against were really good things. There was nothing theologically wrong with it. But in the end, we simplified it to "God is good. He is who He says He is and His Word is true."

DAY 2 **DEFINE YOUR BRAND**

Have a discussion with a leader or staff member about specific ways they saw your church living the brand. If you don't have a branding statement, start a discussion about what your church would like people to say about it behind its back.

CLARIFY YOUR CALLING

In Ephesians 4:11, we are told of the fivefold ministry of the church. These five offices were appointed that the church would be built up, and all would become mature and attain the fullness of Christ. In this verse, the Bible tells us that some are appointed to be apostles, some to be prophets, some to be evangelists, and some to be pastors and teachers. So not everyone is appointed to be a pastor and not everyone is appointed to be an evangelist. Apostles go. Prophets exhort. Pastors shepherd. Teachers teach. Evangelists connect. As ministry leaders, it is important that we know to which of these offices we are called, and just as important to know to which offices we are not called. It is the heart of the evangelist that burns for those who live far from Jesus. It is in the passion of the evangelist that undiscipled people hear the gospel and connect with the body of Christ.

We in the church are in the relationship business, so the first thing we have to do is connect with people so that they will hear the message of the gospel. To do this, the church leader or pastor has to make an important first decision. *Am I the person on my team who has the burning desire and fiery yearning to reach undiscipled people?* Church leaders have various gifts. Not all pastors or staff members are evangelists. The person at your church whose responsibility is to gather people *must* have the evangelist gift. If we're to complete our mission to make disciples, if we are going to connect with undiscipled people, we have to make sure that the people we appoint to connect our ministries with the neighborhood and community have an evangelist's heart.

To take the steps we outline in this book, first find the person whose desire for connecting the people to the church oozes. Perhaps it sounds daunting to add one more person. But remember that a church only needs about five people to complete the fivefold ministries. The gifts are there in your church. Here's how you find them. Let's say your church started to shrink.

"WHO WOULD BE BROKENHEARTED ABOUT THE PEOPLE WHO ARE NOT GOING TO MEET JESUS? YOU WANT THAT EVANGELISTIC PERSON TO BE PART OF THE CONNECTION PROCESS AT YOUR CHURCH."

Who would be worried about whether you could keep the lights on and pay the bills? Who would be concerned about the reputation of the church and its standing in the community? Who would be brokenhearted about the people who are not going to meet Jesus? You want that evangelistic person to be part of the connection process at your church. That's the one whose heart is breaking when people aren't meeting Jesus. That heart beats in the person who will work tirelessly to connect your ministry with the neighborhood and the community around your church.

The post-Christian church is paying for a late-Christian era phenomenon. At some point, we decided not to appear too aggressive, so we stopped proselytizing. The evangelist on your team needs to be *so* willing to proselytize that the passion of it will sometimes rub other people on the team a little raw. If you don't have someone on your team like this, get one. Perhaps it's a board member or a volunteer.

When you find that person, you want them in leadership. This person can serve as the director of evangelism and outreach or, depending on the size of the church, they may be just responsible for the annual chili festival and vacation Bible school. This person who sees the jewel of a lost soul as the most valuable treasure on earth needs to be part of the process of communicating with the community and neighborhood around you.

In the vast majority of churches, this person is a creative and relational person. They might not be the best at administration or technology. Even though good administration and technology are important, being passionate about bringing people in and making an emotional connection is most important for the evangelist. Everyone else can report to the evangelist and other tasks can be outsourced, but the burning desire to see others find Jesus cannot be outsourced.

The evangelist gift is the gift that draws the crowds. When I was a young Christian, I was invited to be on the evangelism committee of my church. A great saint of God in that church, one of the best Bible scholars I ever heard, said the evangelism committee was like the marketing and advertising committee. I didn't know it then, but now I understand that this was Late-Christian era thinking. The Late-Christian era model was, "Everyone is going to church anyway, and we just need them to come to ours." If people come to church because they are looking for one to attend, then marketing would work. The Post-Christian era model is that much fewer people perceive a *need* to go to church anymore. If our churches don't adjust, then our numbers, our influence, and our mission will continue to shrink.

Today, gathering an audience is the first step in evangelism. In Acts 2, about one hundred and twenty people gathered in an upper room. The Feast of the Harvest was happening right outside, with perhaps a quarter of a million people attending. All of a sudden, tongues of fire fell. People heard their native language being spoken and they were drawn to it. Then Peter went out and preached to the crowd. Three thousand were saved. Note that the first thing God did was to gather a crowd out of a crowd. Disciple-making is done knee-to-knee, one at a time. Most evangelism is done in *groups*.

The group we want to gather needs to be as big as we can possibly make it. God told us to go make disciples of *ethnos*. That word, translated as "all nations" in Matthew 28 means "all people."[1] Only in the last thirty years has connecting with "all people" become technically possible. The creation of the Internet has had a greater effect on our world than the Gutenberg press. Its impact on society is more in order with the discovery of fire or the wheel. The Internet has changed how people connect and how relationships form, especially with institutions.

The new generation is greatly affected by the Internet. A famous leader once said "young people today love luxury, have bad manners, contempt for authority; they show disrespect for elders and love chatter in place of exercise." Sounds bad, doesn't it? Socrates said this in about 400 BCE. We do have a generational problem but it's not a modern problem. The issue that *is* modern, and that didn't affect the young people of Socrates's day, is the Internet.

The Internet's greatest impact is in how relationships are formed especially with institutions. We in the church are in the relationship business, so we have to understand that the Internet has changed relationships and how

---

1James Strong, "Strong's Greek: 1484. ἔθνος (ethnos) -- a Race, a Nation, Pl. the Nations (as Distinct from Isr.)," Biblehub.com, accessed August 16, 2018, www.biblehub.com/greek/1484.htm.

they are formed. We can embrace that the Internet is a tool for evangelizing everyone, yet understand it's also a curse that makes the Devil chuckle.

God said *ethnos*, meaning "all people." If God didn't want a crowd, why did He say "all"? We are the first generation that has the possibility for everyone who is alive today to hear the name of Jesus at the same time. We *can* do that so we have to start living like people who *can* do that. If it's possible to evangelize everyone on earth at the same time, then we need to at least start evangelizing everyone in our neighborhood or town. In the part of earth that we occupy, we need to start gathering the "raw materials": the crowds, to be evangelized. This starts by choosing the hearts (evangelists) who will lead the drive.

DAY 3 CLARIFY YOUR CALLING

Identify at least one person in your church with an evangelist's heart and meet with them. Ask them to dream with you on how you can reach your community and neighborhood. Then together, try and turn one of those dreams into reality.

KNOW YOUR AUDIENCE

Church growth statistics tossed around today place the average American church attendee in a pew about once a month. The more startling statistic is that when we are in church on Sundays, seventy-nine percent of our neighbors aren't.

To know your audience, consider that on any given Sunday, eighty percent attending are the regular attendees and twenty percent are the non-regulars. That twenty percent adds up. When I share this number with pastors and ministry leaders it usually mirrors their personal experiences. A better way to put it is that twenty percent of the seats your church fills in any given week are filled by people who come to your church less than once a month. But have you ever wondered this over a course of a year? How many unique individuals does it take in a given year to fill the seats you fill on Sundays?

Usually, when I try and explain the math behind these numbers, most people start looking at their smartphones. But the math behind this is powerful, and the impact of understanding it for your church is profound. Please stay with me here.

Let's say a given church gets 100 people each Sunday in worship, never more, never less. Eighty people come more than once per month and twenty come less than once a month. That means this church fills 5,200 seats per year (100 X 52= 5,200). However, to calculate how many unique individuals it takes to fill these seats requires that we know the average number of visits per month for each group.

I run a charity (TheProvisumGroup.com) that manages churches and faith-based charities all over the United States. Some of our church clients take attendance every week and we keep those databases for some of them.

Once a year we take all that data and put it into one database and "do the math." I can tell you that all the people who attend one or more times a month average 2.75 visits per month (33 visits per year). People who attend less than once a month average .2 visits per month. Now in this group of less-than-once-a-month visitors are all the "one and dones" too. These are the people who come one time (like to visit Grandma at Christmas) and do not return again in that same year. Regardless, as a group they average .2 visits per month (which is 2.4 visits per year).

The table below illustrates how many unique individuals it takes to fill 5,200 seats per year (100 people in worship times 52 weeks = 5200 filled seats per year) where eighty percent of the seats are filled by people who average thirty-three visits per year and twenty percent of the seats are filled by people who average 2.4 visits per year.

	PERCENT OF WEEKLY WORSHIP	SEATS FILLED PER YEAR	GROUP AVG. VISITS PER YEAR	UNIQUE INDIVIDUALS PER YEAR	PERCENT OF TOTAL
12+ VISITS PER YEAR	80%	4160	33	126	22.54%
11- VISITS PER YEAR	20%	1040	2.4	433	77.46%
TOTAL	100%	5200		559	

Over the course of a year, the actual number of casual, non-regular attendees equals about seventy-five percent of the unique individuals who walk through your doors. Or stated differently: For every person who attends your church more than once per month, there are 3.43 people who attend less than once per month. This is why the "membership" numbers of most churches soar by comparison to the "regular attendee" numbers.

Catch the weight of this: About seventy-five percent of the people who walk through the doors of your church over the course of a year attend your church less than one time per month. How will you disciple them? How will you even get them to come back? Think about your church communications. To start with, how much common knowledge can you assume everyone who attends your church possesses? How can we assume that people who attend a few times a year possess the same knowledge about what is happening at the church as people who attend every week? How do we communicate with both groups? Does our communication work for both groups? If people are coming less than once each month, what kind of communication do you need to use to be adequately conveying the information you have?

For example, let's say an announcement is made from the pulpit, "To become more involved, go to the Connections Center after the service." The seventy-five percent people who you've managed to get interested are going to walk out of the service and hunt for a "Connections Center." If all they see is a sign that says, "Welcome," they aren't going to know if it's the right place. What is announced has to be clear, and the follow-up needs good signage and an actual person waiting there to act on the instructions that were announced.

Another common mistake is when the communication from the pulpit, let's say for a church picnic, is "Go see John Campbell." Twenty percent of the people sitting in church that day don't know John Campbell. So your good efforts to have an event to draw in the community are thwarted by assuming they know someone who is in fact a stranger.

A good way to grasp what your people are experiencing is to visit another church — or have a staff member go and report back — and watch the level of communication. Seeing how much common and local knowledge

"ONE BIG REASON COMMUNICATIONS ARE POOR IN MOST CHURCHES TODAY IS THAT THE VAST MAJORITY OF PEOPLE RUNNING CHURCH COMMUNICATIONS ARE THINKING IN TERMS OF THE LATE-CHRISTIAN ERA"

is assumed in most churches might help you adjust the level of communication in your own church.

One big reason communications are poor in most churches today is that the vast majority of people running church communications are thinking in terms of the Late-Christian era. They have Late-Christian era paradigms. That paradigm states that people are wandering into our church because they are looking for a church, and the only question is "which church will they choose." That paradigm says that once people join, they will attend most if not all services. We tend to hire people with this "old church" paradigm because they know how to get things done. We need their expertise, and yet they perpetuate Late-Christian era thinking on our staff, on our board, and when we go out to dinner with them.

Seventy-five percent of the people who walk through your church doors probably don't have that paradigm. They might be in the church building because of a wedding or a funeral. Or maybe it's to honor a parent or see a child's performance. Or it could be a crisis they're going through. But remember, seventy-five percent of those who are coming to your church *do not think* the way the staff person or board member thinks.

Forty years ago, people went to church because "that's what you should do." Going to church was something you *did*. In the post-Christian era, going to church is something you *try*. In the Late-Christian era, people who walked through the doors were looking for a *church*. Today, the people who walk through the doors are looking for an *answer*. I know I keep repeating this but understanding this diversion of paradigms is key to connecting with the community and neighborhood and therefore crucial to growing the church.

In the Late-Christian era, most of the people who walked through the doors of the church were *members* or at least children of members somewhere at some time in their lives. Perhaps they attended Sunday school as kids and received biblical training, so they were already disciples. Today, the people who walk through the doors of the church are *customers* — at least in their own eyes. We don't have to advocate "Christian consumerism"; we just have to understand that's how *they* view themselves.

For people over fifty years old today, many if not most of them went to Sunday school as kids or knew others who did and they understood church to be a place that serves and meets the needs of *others*. The people who visit today are looking to get something for *themselves*. They want to be served. The people who walk through the doors of the church *want their needs met*. As we connect with these people and begin the disciple-making process, these Post-Christian era people begin to learn that self-sacrifice is entry level Christianity. But in this Post-Christian era, *we have to connect before we disciple.*

Years ago, when people decided to join a church, they received many more benefits than just their faith. Some wanted to build social equity. You may have heard how Dwight Eisenhower claimed to be Presbyterian in order to have a church affiliation, just so he could run for president. If you were a life insurance salesperson during that era, you might join the biggest church in town to increase your customer base. If you were running for mayor, you'd want to expand your reach or gain volunteers by joining a church. In other words, there used to be a *social advantage* to joining a church. Today in many places, there is a *social disadvantage* — a stigma instead.

Undiscipled people are the raw materials of disciple-making, so to fulfill the Great Commission to make disciples, we need to connect with *people.* We have to deal with people, and the people we get may not be the ones we want! They might be "what's in it for me" people who are focused only on themselves. Or they may be coming with great social pressure *against* them attending. They may be coming infrequently and cannot be counted on. But we can't serve the people we wish we had. We can only serve those actually come; and more importantly, come back. They're the reason we're here.

Jesus is the One who told us to make disciples of "all" people. Obviously, no one church is going to reach all seven billion people on the planet today. But if we have seventy-five percent of our attendees coming infrequently, then that's where we start. And if seventy-eight percent of the people in your neighborhood are not attending, then that's who we target.

DAY 4 KNOW YOUR AUDIENCE

Pick a current communication and have someone show you how the communication accounts for all people (saints, disciples, community and neighborhood) as well as all levels of attendance. How does it move the neighborhood to community and move community to disciples (being made)?

DAY 5

ASSUME DESIRE

Rule Number One for follow-up is: *Assume the person who gave you contact information has a desire to connect.*

In the Late-Christian era (the second half of the twentieth century) people were reluctant to give out their contact information. They were reluctant

"RULE NUMBER ONE FOR FOLLOW-UP IS: ASSUME THE PERSON WHO GAVE YOU CONTACT INFORMATION HAS A DESIRE TO CONNECT."

for many reasons, but the main reason was the fear of losing control of their information. It was common practice for marketers and list compilers to sell the information they collected, but that is not as much the case in the twenty-first century. There are do-not-call lists; unsubscribe and blocking options; and spam filters. On top of that, there are real consequences for people who exploit these digital channels of communication. In fact, the only place left over which we have no control is our mailbox. Anybody who wants to spend their money on postage and printing are legally allowed to mail us whatever they want.

In the twenty-first century, people wouldn't have given you their contact information if they didn't want to receive follow-up. In the Post-Christian era, there is *no* perceived moral obligation to step inside a church door, and *plenty* of perceived reasons to stay away. The people who visited your church today went because they *wanted* to go. They are looking for something and they are expecting the church to put its best foot forward and reach out. Many times, they are looking for change. Something in their life has become unsatisfying to the point that they are willing to take action and going to church seemed like the right thing to do today.

Maybe they know someone who goes to church and they want a life like someone they know who attends your church or someone else's church. They walk through your doors thinking, *Somewhere in here is the key to what I am looking for.* We know that Jesus is the answer and it is the job of your communications and outreach teams to connect them to people who will show them the way, and the truth and the life.

One of the churches we work with was taking their follow-up campaign very seriously. We worked with them to develop a six-part drip campaign — meaning that the new person got some type of communication from the church every week for six weeks with a goal of meeting that person's individual needs to provide the opportunity to connect in a more meaningful way; and as a result, have the visitor return.

In that church, as invariably happens, one person argued against sending "so much" communication. This person insisted the communication wouldn't work and why. This is how it went:

Him: Visitors are going to feel like we're hounding them.

Me: They gave us their name because they want us to connect with them. If they don't want us to connect, they can just unsubscribe.

Him: They'll all delete it.

Me: If everyone deletes it, why does our average campaign have a forty percent open rate?

Him: So then sixty percent don't open it!

Me: That would only be correct if you assume that the same forty percent open all six. That's an assumption I don't make.

Him: Well, I delete everything I get like that.

Me: *You* are not *them.*

This simple conversation represents one of the most dangerous precepts left over from Late-Christian era thinking. There are still people in the twenty-first century who are well churched and know what they are looking for in their faith lives. But today, most people don't. The assumption that people visiting churches are well churched, know what they want and will let us know when they are ready to connect is a precept that is separating the church from the neighborhoods and communities with which Christ commanded us to connect. Your church will probably not grow if this twentieth century precept still prevails in your congregation. It's a church killer.

There are three fatal flaws in communications that are exhibited when this precept reigns supreme.

First fatal communications flaw: When these conversations happen, it's generally because the person speaking is saying what they think or feel, not what the data shows. In my book, *Minding His Business*, I taught the important marketing principle, "*You* are not *them.*" It's impossible to overstate the fatal flaw of thinking that others are like us. We are not able to peek inside their brains or see their choices or have the perspective of their background. We do not know why they came. **We are not them**.

Second fatal communications flaw: We cannot assume that a visitor has *no* desire to learn more about what the church has to offer. They *attended!* We asked for their contact info and they gave it to us. Further, for many of these people, we asked for their information *only* *if* they wanted us to follow-up with them. We made a spoken covenant to find out together what God has for their lives (See Chapter 10, page 37 for The Provisum Minute). **We made a promise to see what the Holy Spirit would do through our connection.** For all those reasons, at the very least, we have a moral obliga-tion to contact those who give us their information and make our very best effort to connect them to people in our church.

Third fatal communications flaw: We cannot assume that the commu-nity — the people for whom we have contact information — do not see the church as something they need more of in their lives. Many people are struggling to get up every day to face the problems that drove them to your church. **They *want* our answers**, which is why they've agreed on some level to "give church a try." If they were not interested, they would have unsubscribed.

These assumptions were birthed in the Late-Christian era and are gen-erally carried into the present day by well-meaning, well churched people from that era who attend church because they have convictions or traditions, not because they just feel like it. This kind of person doesn't have to look at a brochure on the "Seven Steps of Salvation" because they already know them. Without even reading it, they could give a good guess.

As our communications pave the way for connection to take place and the disciple-making process to begin, some people will connect for a while. Some will never connect. But some will connect and grow. Some will commit their lives to Christ. In this Post-Christian twenty-first century digital world, if they really did *not* want you to communicate with them, they would *not* give you their e-mail addresses or cell phone numbers. They would unsubscribe or block the church's communication. Most don't.

We need to assume desire. In all our communications, assume that *people want to have something you have*. Assume that if you have their contact information, they want to hear from you. Assume desire.

ACTION STEP
DAY 5 — ASSUME DESIRE

Actively contact one person who recently appeared on your file. Ask that person to describe their expectation. Ask them if their expectation was met. Ask them if you could pray for a specific need for them. Invite them back to the next outreach or connect event.

DAY
6

THE PLATINUM RULE

The Golden Rule is, "Treat others the way you want to be treated."

The Platinum Rule is, "Treat others the way they want to be treated."

Platinum is more valuable than gold.

My three sons were all pretty good athletes. I'd had some athletic success as a kid, so I taught my three sons what I'd learned: The way to get better was to get coached and critiqued. "Winners seek criticism. Champions crave it." That what I taught them.

Throughout my higher education and when I launched into business, I felt that the greatest show of respect and trust someone could give me was to let me know what they thought I was doing wrong. I appreciated those willing to invest in my life by showing me how to do things right. In my mind, it felt like those people were saying they valued me enough to want me to succeed. Winners seek criticism, champions crave it. *But the business world doesn't really work that way.*

For the first fifteen years of my career in senior management and as a CEO of a couple of companies, I felt that I was the living embodiment of the Golden Rule. Everywhere I went, I respected and cared for people enough to criticize their mistakes. I thought it was my duty to criticize in order for people do better. I should have had a clue at some point in those fifteen years that not everyone wanted to be criticized. Unfortunately, I didn't. Eventually, it dawned on me that people didn't want to be treated the same way I wanted to be treated.

Then I attended a seminar in which a speaker taught "the Platinum Rule." He said it was, "Treat people the way *they* want to be treated." When I heard that, all the lights in my head went on. I didn't hear angels singing, but the guardian angels of my employees were probably having a hoedown.

Treat people the way they want to be treated. A fable about a dog and a fish can't pass a physics test, but it illustrates the point. The dog and the fish were best friends. The dog went to the pond every day and frolicked in the water with the fish. One day the dog got a new house, so instead of going to the pond, he invited the fish to his house. To show the fish his best hospitality, the dog pulled down a beautiful wooden box inlaid with mother-of-pearl. He opened it and offered his friend his prime possession: a perfect bone. The fish turned and walked out the door, muttering, "I thought you were my friend!" The problem was, you need teeth to chew on a bone. In all the time they were friends, the dog had never noticed that the fish didn't have any teeth. The fish saw the dog's intended act of respect as insensitive and embarrassing. The fish got its feelings hurt and the dog was confused.

"WE MAKE BONEHEADED MISTAKES LIKE THAT WHEN WE TREAT PEOPLE THE WAY WE WANT TO BE TREATED INSTEAD OF THE WAY THEY WANT TO BE TREATED. "

We make boneheaded mistakes like that when we treat people the way *we* want to be treated instead of the way *they* want to be treated. How do we find out how they want to be treated? We *ask* them. The good news is that church growth experts have done all the asking already. They've conducted surveys and questionnaires in thousands of churches every year. Many of these experts have come up with universal "truths." One that rings true in every church I've worked with is that people who are considering visiting a certain church want the answer to three basic questions:

1. What is the worship service going to be like?

2. Do the people look like me (young, old, children, married, single etc.)?

3. What is going to be done with my children?

They want to know what is going to happen when they visit. What do they get if they commit? What's in it for me? We talked about church Christian consumerism in chapter four. Christian consumerism is not desirable but it is a reality of the Post-Christian era. The sooner we recognize this new truth, the better we will be at connecting with the neighborhood and community.

In your first-time visitor follow-up, your drip campaign, and all your digital marketing and communications, should follow the Platinum Rule and answer the question everyone in the neighborhood and community is asking: *"What is in it for me?"* Spend time asking questions like these: What do they want? What are they looking for? Then integrate the answers into your communications.

For example, what is the primary reason a family chooses to participate in a parent's night out event? Is it because the children will have a great time? Is it because the facilities and staff are world class or is it because the children might learn something about Jesus? All these are good reasons and are probably going to happen. But are these the primary reason a family chooses to participate? Probably not. The answer is more likely that the decision maker (the parent(s)) want a three-hour break, so it is important that all the communication about the parent's night out event include "the three-hour break" idea. All the cool things that the children will experience are the "icing on the cake." The kids may enjoy the magic show, but the decision maker(s) need a break and your "big church full of really nice people who do all that cool stuff" is the one who can give it to them.

It is also important that you communicate with people in the way they want to receive communication. In this digital age, people have shorter attention spans than ever. That means it is better to have a ninety-second video than a three-minute video. But if you need to have a three-minute video, or a long statement, make sure it is very important. If the people don't deem your videos or written pieces as important or valuable enough to invest their time, they won't listen to or read the next one. The fact that you are reading this book means you're already on this path.

I recently volunteered at a parent's night out event. At the end of the evening a young single mom came to pick up her three boys ages one, three, and five. I asked her how she spent her evening. I'm not kidding; this is how she replied: With tears in her eyes, she said "I went to Starbucks. I drank a cup of coffee and the coffee was hot." We asked her if she would repeat that on video so we could use it to promote our next parent's night out event.

ACTION STEP

DAY 6 THE PLATINUM RULE

Review the communication plan for one ministry. Ask these three questions:

1. What needs/desires does this ministry fill?

2. Are those the likely needs or desires our target audience is looking for?

3. Are these needs/desires mentioned in communication plan and pieces?

DAY
7

AM I REALLY GONE?

Most ministries with a database or donor list have a group of people they call "lapsed." These are people who donated or attended in the past but are not giving or attending now. Most churches with a database or membership list have a group of people they remove from communications. These are people who have attended in the past but have not attended in a "long time."

Before we look at that group of people, I'll tell you an embarrassing but extraordinarily enlightening personal experience. Years ago, I attended a seminar about "lapsed donors." One of the speakers said that far fewer people are actually "gone" than the ministry thinks are gone. To prove the point, the speaker gave us an exercise: write down very quickly the five charities you avidly support. If you don't have five, write three, but do it without thinking hard about it. When you get home, check your bank account to see when the last time was that you gave to them.

I immediately wrote my church, Focus on the Family, and a couple of others. Focus had helped me raise my sons. Their ministry gave me a vision of the father and husband God wanted me to be. For that reason, I was an avid Focus supporter. You could ask anyone — and you still can today — what ministry had the greatest impact on my life as a father and a husband and I'd say Focus on the Family. As I wrote these things down, this was just some silly exercise for which I knew the answer, so I didn't get the speaker's point. You have probably already guessed what happened when I got home. I checked my records and found that I had not made any recent donations to Focus on the Family. In fact, I had not given to them in *years*. Yet in my heart, I was still loyal, still passionate, and still felt I was part of the ministry.

Let's bring this back to churches in general. If you ask Americans whether they are Christians or not, a majority will still say yes, even though roughly about twenty-one percent will be in church on Sunday. If you take it further and ask, "Where do you go to church?" Most people will say, "I go to _____" and they'll name a church. Let's bring this down to your church: *Many of the people on your six-to-twelve-months-lapsed list will still say they attend your church.* Are they really gone?

One pastor we worked with was a gregarious, hand-shaking man who lived in and loved the community he served. He talked to everyone. Strangers were just friends he hadn't met yet. As he chatted with people, he would eventually talk about the person's faith. After all, he was the pastor of the biggest church in town. Then he would ask what church they attended. Invariably, many people would name his church. And some of those same people who named his church would then look at him and ask where *he* attended. If they attended, they would know he is the pastor. But they *identified* with the church he pastored even though the last time they attended, there was a different pastor.

There is a difference between "haven't shown up recently" and "gone." When someone hasn't come around, it doesn't mean they are gone. People are not really gone until they've made a decision that they're not coming back. "Haven't shown up recently" usually occurs before "leaving", and both of those are different from *deciding* not to come back. "Attending less," "leaving," and "gone" are three different things.

In Revelation 2:4-5, the church at Ephesus was told to do their first works over again, which was to love God. In the case of the lapsed attendees, it's time to do what you did in the beginning and, in this case, *love them* back into fellowship. Remember the progression. Lapsed folks are still part of your community and should be treated that way. For the person who comes the first time, we start moving them from "community" to disciples. We give them reasons to come back. That is where the Platinum Rule comes in — what do they *want*? The reason why we communicate with them at all is because we *assume desire*.

When you're looking at the people who are six-to-twelve months lapsed (or more) on your records, *assume desire*. Assume they want to be affiliated with you. They just don't want to come back to church today. Your job is

"WHEN YOU'RE LOOKING AT THE PEOPLE WHO ARE SIX-TO-TWELVE MONTHS LAPSED (OR MORE) ON YOUR RECORDS, ASSUME DESIRE."

to use the Platinum Rule and find out what they *want* and then give them a reason to *want* to come back. The best place to start with these folks is probably a phone call from the same people you are using to help new community members connect with your ministry.

God doesn't give up on us. The church should not give up on people either. Keep moving people forward by identifying groups, such as six-to-twelve months lapsed. To fulfill our mission, we constantly move people from neighborhood to community, from community to disciples, and from disciples to saints.

DAY 7 AM I REALLY GONE?

Ask to see a list of people who attended last year, but have not attended in the last six months. Assume their desire to stay affiliated with your church. Now list five things your church can do to possibly make them want to come back. Do one of those things.

DAY
8

FILL THE BUCKET

What if I told you it is possible to double the size of your worship attendance without adding one new person? Think it's possible? Read on.

Think about a bucket with a hole in the bottom. How can you fill it? If you make more water go into the top of the bucket than what is coming out of the bottom, it will fill. In the church, as long as there are more people coming into a church than leaving a church, the pews will fill. This is the most basic church growth strategy you will ever hear.

Let's look at the bucket again, but this time from the bottom. Doesn't it seem like if we could shrink that hole, the bucket would fill easier and faster? Just as it is easier and less expensive to fill a bucket with only a tiny hole, it is far easier and less expensive to get people in your community to return to church than to get new people to come for the first time. So filling the bucket is a combination of getting more of the neighborhood to attend (filling the bucket from the top) and getting the community to come more often (shrinking the hole in the bottom of the bucket) and get people who are coming less to attend more (also shrinking the hole in the bottom of the bucket).

Remember the "community" is one of the four groups of people in a typical church. These are the people for whom you have at least one piece of contact information. The "neighborhood" is the people nearby for whom you have *no* contact information. It is profoundly more expensive to get the neighborhood to come to your church than it is to get your community to return to church or attend more often.

For the neighborhood, because you don't have their contact information, you can only communicate through advertising. Either knock on their door, advertise in a local newspaper, buy an ad on television, radio or in the local movie theater, secure a billboard, pay social media to pinpoint the neighbors, or buy a list and call or mail them. When you reach out to the neighbors, you'll need some reason for them to respond. Perhaps you'll throw a party. We'll detail exactly how to do this later in the book (Chapter 11). All we're saying here is that it's more expensive to fill the bucket from the top than it is to shrink the hole in the bottom.

In most businesses, it's much less expensive and more profitable to re-activate a dormant customer than to get a new customer. Look at a hypothetical church of 200 regular attendees that has a thousand people on their database. That means 800 people do not attend or rarely attend. "Filling the bucket" means getting some of those 800 people to come back and attend more often.

Here are some numbers for you. Looking at that group of seventy-five percent who come to church less than once a month, let's just say they come .2 times per month. If you get that group to average coming to your church once per month, their average group attendance grows from .2 monthly to once monthly.

If you can get the "seventy-five percent" people as a group to average one visit per month, your weekly attendance will almost double. You read it right: almost double.

"IF YOU CAN GET THE 'SEVENTY-FIVE PERCENT'" PEOPLE AS A GROUP TO AVERAGE ONE VISIT PER MONTH, YOUR WEEKLY ATTENDANCE WILL ALMOST DOUBLE. YOU READ IT RIGHT: ALMOST DOUBLE."

Let's say there is a set of grandparents who send their grandchildren to your VBS program but don't always attend (two people), and a single professional woman who couldn't find a life group that accepted her so she rarely attends (one person), and a couple with two teenagers who got mad at the youth leader and now only come on special occasions (four total), and a young couple who disagreed with someone about child-rearing so they sneak in and out to avoid them (five people including the children).

What if these irregular attendees, members of your community, came more often? They are interested in the church. In the past, they have had a vested interest. There is a "should" in them of variable strength that drives them to attend. If you coaxed only these twelve to attend monthly, church attendance would grow by three people every week. Are they worth reaching out to? Absolutely.

We're going to drill down on ways to draw those people back into relationship, and "close the hole" in the bottom of the bucket in later chapters. For now, the important thing is for you to understand that by shrinking the hole, your church attendance can almost double .

DAY 8 FILL THE BUCKET

Ask to see a list of people who attended twelve times or more last year and have not attended once in the last ninety days. Come up with one way to reach out to those people and invite them back in the next fourteen days.

CAPTURE NAMES

In chapter three I mentioned how I believe that the invention of the Internet by order of magnitude has had the same impact on society as the discovery of fire or the invention of the wheel. The Internet has changed how we learn, how we communicate, how we socialize, and most importantly, how we connect. The church that fails to recognize this and adapt its connection methodologies will eventually perish. There is a new connection model in the twenty-first century.

- The Late-Christian era connection model was: evangelize, convert, connect.

- The Post-Christian era connection model is: connect, evangelize, convert.

Since the beginning, almost all relationships begin with the exchange of names. Until the last twenty-five years, the exchange of names was almost always done verbally. "Hello. My name is Don. What's your name?" When we introduce someone to someone else, the first thing we do is identify all parties by the exchange of names; but the Internet has changed this.

One of the major ways the Internet has changed the world is in the way relationships are formed, especially with institutions. In the church relationships used to be formed like this: Someone would start attending a church, they would meet people, and then eventually the church would ask them to fill out a form. In that Late-Christian era when the church was the leading force in a Christian culture, name capture — getting a person's information into a database — came near or at the end of the process. But think about your own life today. When you heard about this book, you probably looked it up, or looked me up online. That's how we live today.

Today, undiscipled people who are visiting your church for the first time (or the first time in a long time) are likely more comfortable giving you their contact information during that first visit than they are connecting with another person and discussing the reasons that brought them to your church today with the nice people at the church's connection center.

In a previous book, *Minding His Business*, I explained how capturing names, meaning connecting with people, is now the "tip of the spear" of evangelism.

"CAPTURING NAMES, MEANING CONNECTING WITH PEOPLE, IS NOW THE 'TIP OF THE SPEAR" OF EVANGELISM.'"

When someone starts a relationship with an organization or a merchant on the Internet, there is a process of pulling the person into a relationship through steps of engagement or a sales funnel. But when someone has stepped inside your physical church building, *they are already asking for a relationship* .

This is an extraordinarily important concept for you and your entire connection team to understand. A small percentage of people come to your church for the first time or the first time in a long time because they spent the night at Grandma's house, or promised a friend to hear her sing, or some other reason. The larger percentage is there because they're looking for *something*. Forty years ago, when someone walked through the doors of your church, they were probably looking for a church. Today, they are probably looking for an answer and connection. Our responsibility is to give it to them.

As previously mentioned, I run The Provisum Group (TheProvisumGroup.com) which manages churches and faith-based charities all over the country. One of the services we provide is to come and "mystery shop" a church. We will discuss this in detail in chapter 27. We send people into churches who pose as first-time visitors and we test a church's connection processes. Our visitors come armed with secret cameras and recording devices as well as a questionnaire that describes their experience. One of the questions our secret shoppers must answer is "Did anyone ask you for your contact information?" You might be surprised that over eighty-five percent of the time, the answer to that question is no!

In the past, it seemed invasive to ask for a person's telephone, address, and zip code because it gave the church control, but today a person can turn you off with one click. When the person gives you their e-mail or can log on to your app, they have control of the relationship. As a result, there's a much higher trust level when people give their digital contact information. The younger the visitor, the more this is true.

Today, giving contact information isn't what's intimidating. What's intimidating for many people is talking to a real person. Think of the millennial whose wife drug him to church because they're having marriage problems. Would he rather give his contact information or walk up to a "Connection Center" and talk to people about why he and his wife are visiting your church today? Walking up to real people involves the unknown and uncontrolled. He doesn't know what people will say or do. *What if they want to pray for me? What are they going to say to me? What if they ask the last time I've been in church?* Given the choice, he'd rather give you his electronic information. He can control that connection.

One last point about the Connection Center. When the person walks out the door, if all they did was talk to someone at the connection center and no contact information was captured, they left the point of contact behind. With technology, you can talk to the newcomer the way *you* want, with the timing and frequency that *they* want. With technology, you've given them the control they want. Giving people what they want is usually a good idea, especially when trying to connect with them.

ACTION STEP

DAY 9 CAPTURE NAMES

Ask someone to bring you the list of new names (e-mail addresses count too) that your ministry collected last week. If no one is keeping track of that number, start. Appoint someone to bring you that number every week.

DAY 10

LIKE RECEIVING AN OFFERING

An odd scenario plays out among church staff members today. Let's say that this coming Sunday, one staff member has to ask for an e-mail address or for people to log onto the church app, and the other has to ask for money. Which leader would you rather be? Most people would rather talk about the e-mail address and the church app. Few people enjoy asking friends and neighbors for money.

The odd part is that in a church, most people attending assume that offering plates or buckets are going to be passed. Everyone. Even those who have never attended church before have seen it in a movie. When the plate is passed, everyone is expecting it. Not everyone gives, but no one is offended. People understand this is the way churches are. Everyone understands a church needs money to keep the doors open and the lights on. The person receiving the offering is doing the expected albeit harder thing, but is intim-

"NOT ASKING FOR THEIR CONTACT INFORMATION IS ONE OF THE MOST EXPENSIVE MISTAKES A CHURCH CAN MAKE, ON MANY LEVELS."

idated by it. The person asking for an e-mail or to sign up on the church app is doing the unexpected, but easier thing, and yet asking for contact info in church is most often omitted. Not asking for their contact information is one of the most expensive mistakes a church can make, on many levels .

Let me give you another scenario. A senior pastor decides to attend a denominational conference that will require him to miss a Sunday. He asks the youth pastor to fill in for him in his absence. The next week upon his return, the senior pastor asks the youth pastor how it went. The youth pastor says, "It was great! The Spirit moved, and the people responded!" The pastor asks, "What was the offering total?" The youth pastor says, "It was such a holy service, I decided not to break the mood by receiving an offering." Now, will that pastor ask the youth leader to conduct the worship service again? Probably not for a while.

Let's look at the same scenario but give it a different end. The pastor asks how it went. The youth pastor says the service was wonderful. The pastor asks about the offering total. The youth pastor gives him the total. Then the pastor asks, "How many new names did we collect?" The youth pastor says, "I decided not to break the mood and ask for contact information or show the church app." Now, will that pastor be upset with the youth pastor? Probably not. After all, *who cares?* First of all, if you have the evangelist mentioned in chapter three in place, that person will care!

Now let's look at this scenario again for a completely different reason. Let's talk about the money. To do that, let's climb to the 30,000-foot level and look down. On the way up, every one of us will state emphatically that we *are not about the money.* It's hard to overstate enough that our church is *not* just about an offering or finances. We're completely convinced that we're not about raising funds; we are about *people.* It's the *people* we care about.

From the heights, we look down at the second scenario and see that an opportunity to connect with people was squandered. It was omitted because connecting with people was not deemed as important on this particular Sunday. But in the first scenario, the opportunity to receive money was deemed *critical*. As you read the two scenarios, would you be more upset that the youth pastor didn't receive the offering? Or would you be more upset that he didn't give an opportunity to connect with the new people God brought into the building on that Sunday? The difference is because of that part of us that is still living in twentieth century Christianity. In the twenty-first century, *connecting with people by capturing contact info should be as important as taking an offering.* After all, which is more important to God?

Just think about your church this year. Will the Sunday service include passing an offering plate on fifty-two weekends? Will the service include asking for contact information on fifty-two weekends? I want to be clear here. Asking someone to fill out the "about me" card or going to a connection kiosk is not the same as asking for contact info. Asking for contact info implies we are going to try and connect with you. Please don't get the two confused. Asking for contact information needs to become something we *do*. We're living in a Post-Christian era. Connecting with *people* is how we're going to reach the neighborhood and community around us.

Think of a young woman dragged to church during her college break by her mom. That woman is far more likely to listen to a twenty-minute video you send her called "The Way of Salvation" than to come back on the specific day when you're giving this important message. You can't send her the video if you didn't ask her for her e-mail address when she was right there with you.

Let's get our feet back on the ground and look at hard statistics. Our company is a nonprofit dedicated to helping the local church. One of the things we offer is to maintain church databases. Because we provide this service to many churches, we have tens of thousands of records we can study. We've studied the seventy-five percent of people who attend less than once a month. What we've found is that between a third and a half of those will suddenly come several weeks in a row. Why?

When someone who has not been showing up regularly makes a sudden appearance in church, it is probably best that we assume one thing: They're walking through the door with a big "should" in them. What do I mean by a "should"? Think about the millions of people who go to gymnasiums and workout facilities in the month of January. Why do they go? They have a strong "should" in them. They believe they "should" work out because they engaged in too much Christmas cheer. They have a strong "should" to work off the excess weight the holidays brought on. So strong is this "should" that exercise facilities make most of their annual profits during that one month of January.

When the "seventy-five percent people" start coming regularly (for a while), for many it means they have a big "should" in the form of a need (I know we have discussed this already. It is truly so important that it warrants repeating). Something has happened that makes them believe they need to come to church. They need a spiritual lift and they need it *now*. Perhaps they received a bad diagnosis, or discovered a cheating spouse, or can't handle a wayward child, or they lost their job. They're so desperate that they're hyper-attuned. They're at a point in their lives where they're looking for spirituality in *everything*. As they walk through the doors of your church, they think that all of the angels in heaven are standing at attention and sing- ing *Glory hallelujah!* They walk in, take their seats, and hang on every word the pastor preaches.

We have developed what we call **"The Provisum Minute."** We ask our clients to allow us to script one minute in every worship service. Understanding this Post-Christian era concept, we recommend to our clients that they say the following in every service:

> *"If you're here today for the first time, or for the first time in a long time, and something inside you says that right at this moment, you need to do something, and you need to take a step, but you don't know what that step is, I'm going to ask you to do something. Just give us your e-mail address, or text 123 to 456. Write it down on a piece of paper. Put it in the offering plate. Leave it on the pew. Throw it on the floor. We'll find it. Allow us to start communicating with you. Don't worry that we'll over-communicate, because everything we do has a one-click unsubscribe, but let us start communicating with you about what's going on at this church. And together, let's just see what God does."*

Of course, "text 123 to 456" means you have a text campaign with real numbers so they can text to get connected. At The Provisum Group, we can set this up for you.

The data shows that if the "seventy-five percent people" are never engaged when they come back for several weeks in a row, they'll stop coming. Based on the data, the pattern is that they'll miss a few Sundays, then come back one week, miss a few, come back again, and finally leave for good. They're no longer "seventy-five percent people"; they're zeros. Gone. Why? Because they didn't get what they were seeking. Nobody connected with them. People who come to church are looking for connection. Get this in your spirit and in the spirit of everyone you lead .

Let's just say that when the "seventy-five percent person" came back, it wasn't yet time for the all-church study, or the life groups were on hiatus, or the church just finished a major outreach so the staff decided not to push. If *anything* caused the church not to connect, when those precious souls walked in saying "I need help," that opportunity was squandered. This wouldn't be acceptable to the evangelist in our midst, and it shouldn't be acceptable to any of us. The truth is, we have an opportunity *and a duty* to start ministering on the day the person walks through the door.

We must become convinced that when a person gives us contact information — something about their family, about their children, their marital status, they're saying, *"Communicate with me. Connect with me."* As twenty-first century consumers (because they think of themselves as consumers), they are saying, *"I'm here. I'm taking the next spiritual step."* For them, this is an act of faith. What happens if the church never follows up? The Enemy whispers to the person, saying, *"Church people are snobs,"* or, *"God doesn't care about you."*

We'll become far better stewards of the relationships God has given us if we will treat name capture with the same importance as we treat offerings. The challenge in this Post-Christian era is to put as much care into the stewardship of a person's contact information as we do in the stewardship of the finances they entrust to us. Why? Because the money they give is nothing in comparison to the stewardship that is required when they hand us their eternal soul.

ACTION STEP

DAY 10 LIKE RECEIVING AN OFFERING

During your service planning time, appoint someone to make the appeal for contact information in the next worship service(s). Then verify they did as instructed.

DAY
11

THROW A PARTY

Most churches are trying to grow. Sadly, most are not. In order to grow, one thing that has to happen, is the church has to interact with more people. Then we need to connect with those people by first capturing their contact info and then reaching out to them. To use our metaphor, the church needs to start putting more water into the top of the bucket. This is why one of the first questions I ask a church I'm serving is, "How many names are on your database?" This is not a membership or money question. It's an evangelism question. The answer indicates how engaged the church is with the community and neighborhood. If a church that gets 200 for worship has 400 names on the database, it's not doing much to engage the neighborhood. Generally speaking, a church needs about two to three times as many names on their database as they get in worship just to support worship attendance. Remember: For every unique individual who visits your church more than once a month, about 3.43 unique individuals attend less than once a month. If that same church with 200 in worship was doing a decent job of evangelizing the neighborhood and creating community, I would expect them to have 1,000-1,200 names on their database.

If we are going to grow our database, we have to capture names from the neighborhood (people for whom we have no contact information). To "reach" the neighborhood we have to use media (signs, door hangers, advertisement, social media, target marketing or knock on doors) to invite the neighborhood to "come" and "connect." As such, we have to have something to invite them to. I call those "reach events." What makes a "reach event" unique is using media to reach people for whom you have no contact info. I recommend reach events be non-religious — and involve food. Non-religious because we want people who live far from Jesus to come. Food because everyone eats and likes good food. Remember, the order of discipleship for today: Connect, evangelize, convert. In most cases, the neighborhood is not going to be evangelized until they've first connected . Remember also that people are the raw materials needed to fulfill the mission of disciple-making. For the time and money invested, you want to make as many connections with as many people as possible.

How much you spend on your party or reach event depends on your budget. If your church has a large outreach budget, you can do just about anything: a chili cook-off, a carnival, a car show. Let's say the church has no money and no young people. That church can have a Parent's Day Out or Date Night and let the young parents in the neighborhood drop off their children for a couple of hours with kindly grandparents at the church to watch them. Or, you can show the movie *Dumbo* or *Cinderella* in the sanctuary for the kids and grill some burgers in the parking lot, so the young parents can sit around, drink sweet tea, relax, and meet each other.

One of my favorite neighborhood reach events for a church on a tight budget is a food truck festival. You invite a conglomeration of food trucks to your parking lot and let them set up shop. Food truck festivals are fun for the whole family and appeal to a wide spectrum of people. Even better, food trucks will partially pay you back a percent of their revenue for the day. Many of them won't end up paying you the full amount owed, so you have to go into it with your eyes open. But because you get some return income, a food truck festival is less expensive than other kinds of parties. Your expenses will involve a generator, some porta-potties, whatever name-capture materials you may need, and some advertising. (The Provisum Group can help you get door hangers to canvas the neighborhood for a few pennies per household.)

Your reach event needs to be FREE to the neighborhood, but you want to capture names. To do that, we suggest you place orange vinyl construction fencing around the entire party and create "choke points" — openings

"YOUR REACH EVENT NEEDS TO BE FREE TO THE NEIGHBORHOOD, BUT YOU WANT TO CAPTURE NAMES."

in the fence that people will funnel through. Make as many entrances as you can adequately staff for the entire day, so the neighborhood doesn't get discouraged by long lines or tempted to hop the fence. At the entrances, your smiling gatekeepers will offer a paper wristband to attendees once they "text 123 to 456" or write down their e-mail address, or even sign up on the church app. I've seen a food truck festival result in as many as 3,000 new names in a day.

In the first thirty-six hours after your reach event, you can expect thirty to forty percent of the people whose names you collected to unsubscribe or bounce (fake e-mail addresses). But sixty to seventy percent won't. That group is your target for follow-up. Remember what happened on the Day of Pentecost. We are making a crowd out of a crowd (Acts 2). Make sure you have a prerecorded video ready to go, thanking them for coming to your event and inviting them to the next worship service. Also make sure you have a group of volunteers standing by to input all the new contact info you collected into your database and/or your e-mail platform. Then start sending them your weekly e-newsletter.

How this works in real life is best illustrated by a wonderful story that happened to a dying suburban church. Back in the 1950s and 60s, this neighborhood church grew to about 400-500 in worship. That was a huge church in those days. When I was called in a few years ago, which was more than forty years after their peak, the church was down to about sixty people in worship, mostly seniors, and the church was broke. They didn't have a website or social media. They didn't even have a spreadsheet with members' names. Nothing had changed year after year except for when a parishioner died. Over the years, their predominantly white middle-class neighborhood had become an ethnically-mixed, working class neighborhood of young families of a different race. The church had never adjusted to the times. Now they had a huge gap generationally, racially, and culturally with their neighborhood.

The pastor wanted to know what to do, so I told him to go out and find $500. He couldn't imagine how he could find $500 from his members. I advised him, "You cannot be sure that there are not ten saints who have been praying for revival in this church for the last thirty years. Find them and ask them for the money." He did. They gave. With the money, we had a huge vinyl sign made very inexpensively, white with big dark blue letters that spelled out "FREE COOKOUT THIS FRIDAY." The church was geographically situated so everyone in the neighborhood had to pass by the church to get in and out of the neighborhood. We moved the sign around for a week to face different directions in order to ensure everyone saw it.

That Friday, the church brought in someone's grill, got some hamburgers and hot dogs, and had ten of the saints on hand just to love the people who came. The first night, fifteen people showed up for free food, mostly young parents and some kids. Seeing who he'd attracted, the pastor asked for another $500 to purchase basketball hoops. When he got to church on the following Sunday, someone had already put up the hoops in the parking lot. The church kept advertising their free food and started a three-on-three pick-up basketball tournament. It grew. Today, every Wednesday night the church has eighty to 100 people come for a free meal, basketball (weather permitting), and a short Bible study.

Next, we helped with their website, name capture and e-welcome series. An e-welcome series (sometimes called a "drip campaign") is three-to-five pre-produced e-mails with video, thanking people for coming and high-lighting the ministries' best attributes.

Today, that church has a spreadsheet with about 1,000 names. But that's not all they have. One Sunday, a check for $15,000 landed in the offering plate. In the notes section on the check were two words: "Well done!" They hadn't had air conditioning in fifteen years, but they were able to get it working. Then another big check landed in the offering plate. They opened an area of the church that had once been used for children's ministry, but had been locked and chained off because of mold. They got a work crew after it with bleach and paint. Suddenly young families started showing up on Sundays. The next Easter they had a neighborhood Easter egg hunt with over 500 kids participating. Today they have two weekly worship services and a Wednesday night fellowship and Bible study. They're still growing and they've also managed to put $100,000 in the bank. Their average at-tendance on Sunday mornings is 150 people of all backgrounds and ages.

A final note about free food: One church we serve is a fast-growing urban congregation. They shut down their free food pantry because they realized it communicated the opposite of what the church stood for. What the church thought it was saying was, "We care about you." But what the neighborhood was hearing was, "You think I'm poor because I'm _____." (You can fill in the blank with anything.) The food bank *in the recipient's mind* underscored their perceived lot in life. Instead, the church started a community meal once a week. It took off. The message the church now sends is, "We care about you so much that we want to invite you over for dinner and get to know you." And by the way, they are fast-growing because they are *stringent* about capturing names and follow-up.

*Remember, to grow your church you have to meet new people and invite them to come. Then you need to get them to connect. Reach events are the best way to do both.

ACTION STEP

DAY 11 THROW A PARTY

Review the plan for the next reach event designed to get the neighborhood to come. At a minimum, you should have one reach event per quarter.

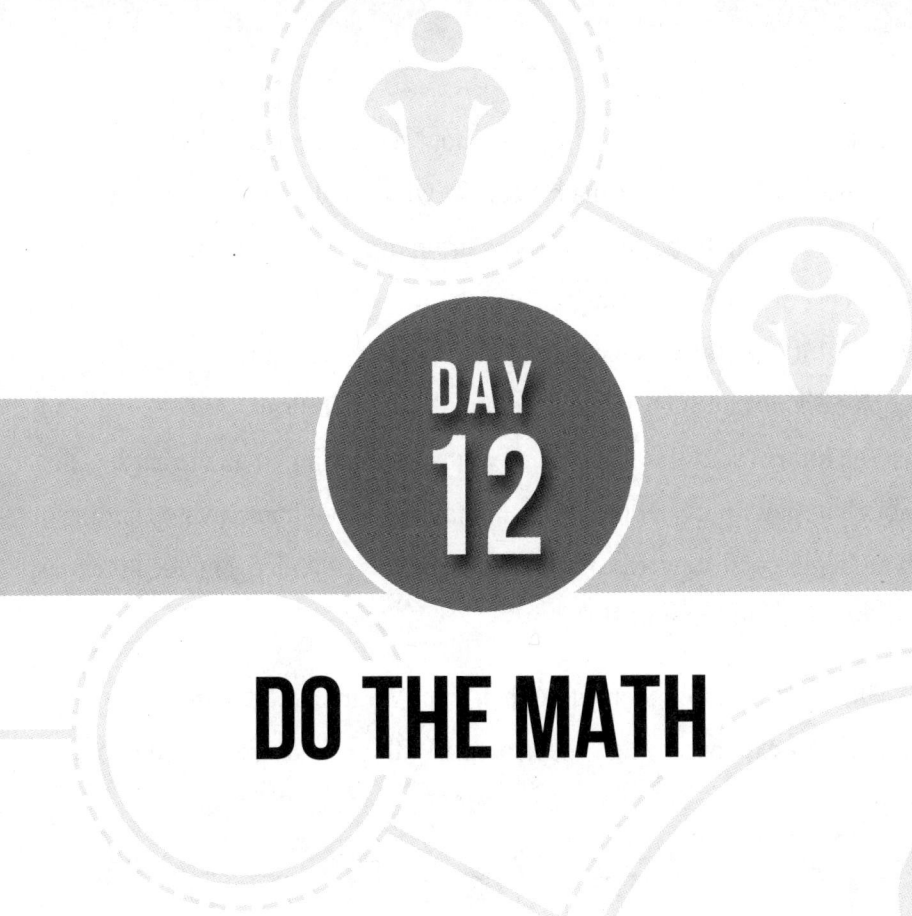

DO THE MATH

This is the chapter when we talk about doing the math, which is *business*. We don't talk about math because we're "all about the money." We talk about the math because finances are required to fulfill our mission in the twenty-first century, and because the mission will generate finances if we fulfill it effectively. Understand that when we talk about "investing" in people, it's not to put a value on a human soul. In Psalm 49:7-8, we read that the human soul's worth is so great that everything in all the earth is not enough to pay for even one. We're not talking about human value here, but about being good stewards of the *funds* God has provided, and the potential *disciples* we can bring to Him.

The first thing to understand when you "do the math" is the difference between an expense and an investment. With an investment, we expect a

"THE FIRST THING TO UNDERSTAND WHEN YOU 'DO THE MATH'" IS THE DIFFERENCE BETWEEN AN EXPENSE AND AN INVESTMENT."

return. If we were to invest in the stock market, we would want to know if it produces a return. Give me a thousand dollars to invest for you, and the first thing you'll ask is what rate of return you can expect. The second question is when you will would get the return.

Let's look at your church outreach budget. Remember, *outreach* is intended to reach your *neighborhood* — the people for whom you don't have contact information. Most churches treat outreach as an expense. In this chapter, I'm going to challenge you to look at it as an investment instead. Remember, the expense is *spent*, but with an investment you expect *a return*.

To understand how the outreach budget ceases to be an expense and becomes an investment, every church leader needs to know two numbers: the "conversion ratio" and the value of a "new name." The conversion ratio is not how many people give their hearts to Jesus. The conversion ratio deals with how many newcomers go on to become members, covenant partners, or whatever is the highest level of affiliation your church has.

We've already established that closing the hole in the bucket means getting your "community" to come to church more often. We'll come back to that later. For now, let's look only at reaching the "neighborhood" using the advertising and marketing budgets for outreach. Let's say that you want to reach out to the neighborhood with an advertising campaign. When you advertise, you need something special to invite them to attend, so you plan a party. (We just talked about "throwing a party" in chapter 11.)

Here is how you get to the two numbers you need to know. Let's say your church has a food truck festival and 500 people attend. Let's say you follow the plan and end up capturing 200 new names and e-mail addresses. These are now new "community" members. That 200 people becomes your denominator. To come up with your ratio, we need to figure out what percentage of those 200 are church members three years later. You may have to go back in church records to figure out what you've accomplished with previous "parties" that you've thrown. Let's say that three years later you retained five percent out of that 200 people. That's ten people or three families. In many churches, that's a nice increase. That five percent is your conversion ratio.

Now, let's do the money math on those 200 new e-mail addresses you captured. Let's say that forty to sixty of those new people hit "unsubscribe" in the first thirty-six hours after the party and you never see them again. That is about average. Let's say that all total 120 people never come back to the church even one more time. That's worse than average. But let's say fifty people (twenty-five percent) come back at least once (two-to-ten visits including the initial reach event) over the next three years and drop a couple of dollars in the offering plate each time they visit. That group collectively will give about $1,000 over three years. Let's say that some other people engage with you, and twenty people (ten percent) return eleven to twenty-four times over the next three years. Each time, they drop ten dollars into the offering plate. That totals collectively $3,200 you've received from this group over the next three years

Out of those 200 people, let's say that ten people (five percent) end up as tithing members, sitting in the front row. Over the next three years, that group collectively gives a total of $13,000. Adding that with the other less frequent attendees from the original 200, the church has received in three years a total of $17,200 from the group of 200 people who the church had never met before. To determine the value of capturing a name, divide the $17,200 by the 200 new people who originally attended the "festival" and gave you their contact information, and you have a new name value of $86. The three-year value of a new name is $86.

VISITS OVER A 3-YEAR PERIOD	PEOPLE	CONTRIBUTION OVER 3 YEARS	3 YEAR VALUE PER NEW NAME
1	120	$0	$0
2-10	50	$1,000	$20
11-24	20	$3,200	$160
24+	10	$13,000	$1,300
	200	$17,200.00	$86.00

To show how it works, let's do this. In the real-world data we manage, the average value of a new name is about eighty dollars. Now just for fun (and verification) take a look at the top 50-100 givers in your church and see how many of them appeared on your roles for the first time in the last three years. I think you will be surprised at how accurate this concept is.

If the food truck festival cost the church $2,000, and you received $17,200 over the next three years, that's an investment with a good return. It's good stewardship. When I work with a church that is unsure of a making an investment in outreach over putting their money into a savings account, I offer them a deal. I tell them I'll give them $2,000 to have their food truck festival if they'll split the giving for the next three years of all the new names they collect at the "festival" with me. Of course, no one ever takes me up on it. Those who are afraid to spend that kind of money, but do it anyway, generally receive back the $2,000 within nine months or less. And over three years, they receive the $17,200 or more. Plus they've grown the church numerically with new members. Ten new members attending every week increases attendance in most churches by about ten percent. And the most important thing to remember is that this is the result of only one festival. What if we had two or three or four outreach events per year for the last five years?

After the average church recovers the expenses, they receive a 126-percent return on their investment every year for the next two-and-a-half years. Many churches try to invest with bank CDs and savings accounts when actually, if we'll just do what we're supposed to do, which is reach out to our neighborhoods, we will get an even greater return — not only in terms of new converts and larger churches, but also in terms of finances. The expression, "Money follows ministry" is an absolute truism.

What does this mean for investment versus expense? Whereas advertising in the twentieth century was put into the "expense" category, using advertising as for outreach for gathering a crowd for evangelism can be put into the "investment" category.

The move from expense to investment is a Post-Christian era phenomena. Investing in people is how we'll evangelize the world. Investing in people is how we'll fulfill our mission to make disciples of "all" people. If you can get this concept into your heart, if you can get to the place where you don't just know the investment in outreach pays off, but you "own" it, your church will grow (or grow again).

DAY 12 DO THE MATH

Have someone calculate the conversion ratio and value per new name for your church. If you need some help, give me a call.

DAY
13

REVIEW THE CALENDAR

Many people walk into your church in a spiritual moment. In their hearts, they say, *God, if You're there, I'm going to this church because....* Sometimes they walk in excited about the possibilities. Sometimes they walk in nervous and anxious because they don't know anyone. But then you ask for their name and e-mail address with a promise to help them figure out how God can meet their need. They give you the e-mail address. They get

"THE MOMENT THEY SHOW UP TO HELP IS STILL THEIR SPIRITUAL MOMENT. THEY ARE STILL RESPONDING TO THAT STILL SMALL VOICE SAYING, 'DO SOMETHING.'"

communications from you. Then they step up to help for an hour to sweep a stairwell. *The moment they show up to help is still their spiritual moment. They are still responding to that still small voice saying, "Do something."*

Remember, the good works that come from volunteering are a *byproduct* of serving. The money raised, the underprivileged kids helped, the missionaries served are all very, very good; and yet they are a byproduct of something larger happening. That is, a new person came to church and *made a connection that leads them to be evangelized.* Why would this be more important than the good work being done? Because serving is part of the disciple-making process. The church is fulfilling its mission to make disciples, and those disciples will make good things happen again and again: money raised, underprivileged children helped, missionaries served. A disciple is being made and that is why the church exists. That is why we are here.

A large church we serve takes a group of teenagers to Mexico every year during spring break. The teens sleep on the floors, eat casseroles, and complete various tasks to help poor people. Some very smart youth leaders divide the young people into work groups before they go. The teens all eat together, but they work in their assigned group all week.

These smart leaders choose their groups based on the teenager's perceived social status. They couple the kids with lesser social status with the kids who have tons of it. For example, they'll put an audio-video nerd with a football quarterback. They pair the homely teenager who hasn't outgrown her dolls with the head cheerleader. What happens? These young people connect. The youth leaders at that church can tell you one teary story after another of the week ending with a popular kid crying to the unpopular kid, "I'm sorry for the way I've treated you. I'll never do that again."

These connections happen to young people on a work trip, to people digging a ditch for an hour, or painting a house for a day. Connections like these often don't happen anywhere else. These kids then go back to their schools and the other kids see how they treat each other. They see the football player eating lunch with the AV kid. They see the modest plain Jane hang out with the cheerleader. They see the body of Christ. This is one way the world is evangelized.

It was Jesus who said, "For you always have the poor with you" (Matthew 26:11a). Why will there never be an end of people in need? One reason is that serving others is one way Jesus fills our hearts with compassion. And compassion is a very important characteristic of a disciple of Jesus. Service to others is how we connect with each other. It is one of the most important ways the body of Christ is built. It is the church's responsibility to make sure this process happens continuously.

If the neighborhood and community look at your church calendar, will they see opportunities for them to serve or connect? If they look at your communication, will they see people being served? It is the church's responsibility to facilitate people serving people. It is church leadership's responsibility to make sure we are always serving others and that the world sees us doing it. What about your church? Take a look at your church calendar. Are you proud of what you see?

Looking at volunteerism through an old lens that measures results of jobs done will cause a church to wither. Looking at volunteerism through the new lens of people making connections causes a church to thrive. Sometimes the only way a person will stay around long enough to see Jesus is to see him through the life of a saint when they connect during an opportunity to serve.

DAY 13 REVIEW THE CALENDAR

Review the next ninety days on your ministry's calendar. Highlight the opportunities for:

1. The neighborhood to come (reach events).

2. The community to connect (connection events).

3. Everyone to serve.

DAY 14

FOLLOW-UP

It's Day 14 and you're already a champion. You have changed this Sunday's order of service to include a time to capture contact information, and your team is excited. But what happens to those names? A while ago, my wife and I got together for dinner with old friends who retired in a coastal state. They had finally settled on becoming members of a very young church. Each week people streamed through the doors to hear very loud contemporary music. The warehouse where they met wasn't full, but most were millennials.

They asked about my work, which is generally not interesting enough to share at a dinner party (not many people get excited about church operations); but when I explained the concept of this book, and hit on the subject of follow-up, they leaned forward — *fascinated.*

What I learned was that they loved to invite people to church. At the restaurants, golf courses, and stores they visited in their new hometown, they invited young people to their new "hip" church. One day they happened across one of the young women whom they had invited, so they asked if she liked the church. She said, "Yes, I gave them my phone number but no one ever called. So *I guess they didn't really care."*

Not long after, they ran into another young person, who, when they asked, *said the same thing!* This church was filling up the top of the bucket, but the bottom of their "bucket" didn't have just a hole — it had no bottom at all. It was more like a tube than a bucket. People were filing through the church and disappearing without anyone asking why!

Because even though this church was attracting young people, it was acting like a leading force in a Christian culture. There was no plan to follow-up. Everything we have discussed (and hopefully you have done up to this point) is a waste if you do not have follow-up.

Remember the maxim: "Begin with the end in mind." I recommend that churches have an entire follow-up campaign prepared *before* starting the

"I RECOMMEND THAT CHURCHES HAVE AN ENTIRE FOLLOW-UP CAMPAIGN PREPARED BEFORE STARTING THE CAMPAIGN TO CAPTURE NAMES."

campaign to capture names. It's great that you're launching initiatives, but before you take the first step, do all you can to ensure your church has an airtight, bulletproof, well-thought-out follow-up plan.

The first thing I suggest you do is create an electronic newsletter that is electronically distributed each week. (You can go to www.connectand-growyourchurch.com/enewsletter to see examples). Every new name captured should be put on the e-newsletter distribution list. You don't have to ask for their permission. They expected you to start communicating with them when they gave you their contact information. This is a twenty-first century concept. The visitor is in control of who contacts them. When they are done, they will unsubscribe.

It is important to note that an electronic newsletter is *not* a pdf of your weekly bulletin. An electronic newsletter is a series of direct links *back to your website*. It drives traffic to your website and distributes the links for redirected marketing.

The electronic newsletter is laid out in the order of discipleship, with the events for the neighborhood and community at the top and the items for the saints and disciples on the bottom. Also, when deciding what goes into the electronic newsletter, you will have to get used to disappointing some people. You are just going to have to ask the eight men in the chess club to call the other members of the club on the phone instead of advertising in the bulletin fifty-two Sundays a year. *This is extremely valuable marketing space!* Communications that impact relatively small numbers of people should be sent via group e-mails and/or texts.

Redirected marketing links are a twenty-first century creation. You know: when you look at a pair of shoes online and for the next week you see those very shoes on your e-mail, social media, and your home page? Everywhere you go, there are those shoes. What happened was that when you visited the original shoe store (website), a small piece of code was added to your laptop or smartphone. We can use this same technology to inform your neighborhood and community (and disciples and saints for that matter) of what is going on in your church. Redirected marketing and social media advertising has almost eliminated the need for traditional media advertising (newspaper, radio, television) at a considerably lower cost. If you are not familiar with this technology, give us a call at The Provisum Group. We set these campaigns up all the time.

Next, I suggest you create a multi-video welcome series that is also distributed once a week. The videos do not have to be highly produced. If all you have is a smartphone with a decent camera that will do. Then put every new name you receive in the welcome series. There are lots of simple software that will help you manage this process. Remember, if a picture is worth a thousand words, a video is worth ten thousand. One of the modern day precepts in marketing in the twenty-first century is that "nobody reads." Now obviously people still read. You are reading this book. But when you are going through your e-mails, if you have a ninety-second video from the pastor of the church you just visited or a 225-word letter, which are you more likely to "open" first?

A sample welcome series could be:

Video 1 ninety second "Thanks for coming" from the pastor that includes an invitation and button to connect on social media

Video 2 two minutes from the children's minister

Video 3 ninety seconds from the missions team showing all the cool stuff your church does to help others

Video 4 ninety seconds inviting them to upcoming event(s)

The whole purpose of the welcome series is to:

1. Start telling your brand story (see chapter 2).

2. Give people reasons to come back.

3. Make connecting simple, instantaneous, and easy.

The welcome series videos should be played on a nested page on your website (not on youtube or Vimeo). On the nested page below the video should be tabs to link to the top upcoming events in your church. If the video being played is from the children's minister, then the tabs should promote VBS or parents' night out. We will talk about these events in Chapter 16 (Provide Connections). For now, you can go to: www.connectand-growyourchurch.com/nestedvideo to see an example of a nested video and connection points like I just described.

Going to church is a decision much like going out to eat. First you decide if you want to make dinner or eat out. Then you decide what you want to eat. Then you decide where you go to eat. The welcome series helps with the "what." If people see "what" they want in your communication, the "where" takes care of itself.

Let's talk about some rules and regulations regarding follow-up.

Follow up needs to be quick. If the follow-up series is already produced, there is no reason the first e-mail can't go out within twenty-four hours. The same day would be better. Once a name is in the welcome series, all the communication thereafter can be preprogrammed to automatically be sent on a prescribed day at a predefined time.

Most churches don't follow-up because nobody cares enough to do the work. That's why great follow-up will set your church apart from most of the others. Follow-up needs to answer "What do I get?" and "Why should I come?" Follow-up says, "We care about you!" Follow-up says, "This church is alive." A lack or absence of follow-up tells people that your church has nothing going on and nobody cares.

DAY 14 FOLLOW-UP

Have someone bring you the list of people receiving each follow-up piece in your new name connection series this week. Then review one follow-up piece. Discuss if the piece needs to be edited or replaced.

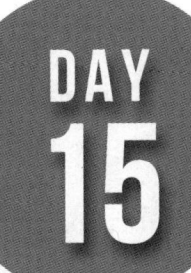

DAY
15

THE DRIP CAMPAIGN

To the question, "How many names are on my database?" a 200-member church may say it has 400 names on the database. That means it's not doing much to engage the neighborhood. If a 200-member church has 4,000 names on the database, it's doing a great job engaging, but it might have a problem with follow-up and connection. In other words, the people who walk through the door are not getting an opportunity to take the next step. They are not connecting.

Let's talk about creating a "drip campaign." A drip campaign is a pre-produced, multi-piece communication strategy designed to engage new people on your file and guide them toward connection. This should last from four to seven weeks and includes four to seven videos. During this time, we hold the new people out of general communications, so they don't get an invitation to engage in the work of the church, like disciple-making.

Following the old adage that *you only get one chance to make a first impression*, the drip campaign should be the best production value your

"THE DRIP CAMPAIGN NEEDS TO BE ONE OF THE BEST COMMUNICATION PACKAGES YOU HAVE PRODUCED IN A VERY LONG TIME."

church can provide. It needs to be better than your best worship service, have the same or better production value than your Christmas program, and be as warm as the pastor's handshake on Sunday morning. The drip campaign needs to be one of the best communication packages you have produced in a very long time. It needs to offer tangible opportunities to connect and answer the three questions we listed:

1. What is church going to be like?

2. Do the people look like me?

3. What are you going to do with my children?

Below is a good overview of a church drip campaign:

Drip 1: The first message — preferably a video — *must* be the pastor saying, "Thanks for coming." It would be great if by the time the newcomer gets home from church, an e-mail from the pastor pops in, saying, "So good to see you in church today!"

Drips 2-4: These need to answer all three questions. The second one might be a longer video, perhaps this can be three minutes with a guided tour of the children's area hosted by the bubbly children's pastor. One "drip" definitely has to be about the children. One of the videos needs to have great shots of people in worship. People singing. People praising, laughing, talking, hugging. Show the world what a great place your church is. Show the community that your church is a place where they will be loved. Show your church living its brand.

Drips 3-5: One early video needs to be about something coming up on the calendar. This can be, "come to something fun," "come and serve," "come and connect" or "come and learn."

"Come do something fun." Every quarter, the church calendar should include something that is just plain fun. We call these reach events. If that's the next thing on the calendar when the person visits, that's what they should be invited to attend.

"Come and learn." One of the bigger "come and learn" attendance in any community is generally a seminar or discussion about child-rearing, and sometimes it's specifically about teenagers.

"Come and connect." If you have a small group program, here is where you tell people about it. One of the sad realities of living in a twenty-first century digital age is that as a society, we are fragmenting. We are becoming disconnected from each other. Many people are lonely and looking for connection. Offer them a way to connect in small groups.

"Come and serve." As we discussed earlier in this book, serving together is one of the best opportunities for people to connect. The service opportunities identified in your drip campaign should be one-time opportunities to serve that are limited to a couple of hours and can be done on one evening, or better yet, on a weekend.

The "come and serve" step can be anything: rake leaves, shovel snow, cook, serve a meal, a clean-up day, help with a festival. Remember, this opportunity is for your newest community member to work alongside someone from the church and make a *connection*. It just has to be kid-friendly and have childcare. For example, a five-year-old can tag along while a parent picks up trash or sweeps a staircase. But for younger children, you have to provide childcare. The childcare itself can be a "come and serve" next step. Young people, young parents, or grandparents can volunteer for an hour or two of childcare while people are serving elsewhere. Remember, everyone's service is limited to an amount of time — one or two hours. Any church can create these quarterly, monthly, or even weekly by adopting the street where the building is, or a nearby elementary school, and inviting people to help clean or beautify it.

Drips 4 through 6: The next-to-last part of the drip campaign is the "tell-me-how-you're-doing message." After providing the drips with information and opportunities, the pastor is back. The message is something like, "Hello again. I just wanted to check to see how you're doing. I'd love to hear from you, so please click the link at the bottom and update me." The link connects to an e-mail address so *the person replies directly to the pastor.* Of course, this e-mail is monitored by a staff member to ensure the pastor sees it.

Last drip: The very last part of the campaign might say, "Click the link below to schedule a phone call." You've now earned the right to offer them an even greater connection with a telephone appointment. Now, you're in the thick of evangelism.

A word on what happens after someone clicks the "connect" button. All of our work, all of our planning, all of our investment has been for this moment. Someone has responded. This would be the worst place to respond with twentieth century passivity. Schedule a phone call now. When someone in the drip campaign responds to "connect," at that moment, send them to a webpage that has a calendar where they can schedule a call with one of the church's "evangelists" (remember chapter 3: Clarify Your Calling*).* There are many calendar software programs that will help you with this. People are busy. If you call people at random, rather than scheduling a call, you will miss a lot of people. Schedule before you dial.

My church has a community dinner every Thanksgiving. For over a decade, serving at this meal has been my family's Thanksgiving tradition. When the annual meal first started years ago, the purpose was to feed poor, lonely, or homeless people on Thanksgiving. Over time the whole community got involved and now it's an annual *community* meal for 300-500 people with another 100 people serving. Two full teams of cooks and clean-up serve two dinner hours. The first seating is at 12:00 and the second is at 3:00. Today, any one of those teams might be made up solely of people from outside the church. The people from the church are able just to love those people who are volunteering.

Our Thanksgiving goal is not reached when people leave on Thursday full of turkey. Our goal is reached as those people who participated, both serving and eating, show up for a Christmas service, then attend again, and the connection results in evangelism.

When you're creative, there's no end to the "next steps" you can provide for people. Some churches have a prison ministry, others a halfway house. Some have after-school programs or schools for the arts. Many churches have an annual carnival, or Easter or Christmas pageants. Remember that at every "next step" opportunity, you want the saints from the church prepared *just to love people.*

DAY 15 THE DRIP CAMPAIGN

Review the Drip Campaign for new people on your file plus the next "big" thing your church is doing. How many opportunities are offered to connect in those responses? Discuss if that is enough. Do any of the drip pieces need to be updated?

DAY
16

PROVIDE CONNECTIONS

We need to keep people coming back to church if we are going to make disciples of all people. That means, we need to shrink the hole in the bottom of the bucket, and we have to be practical about it. Let's imagine that your congregation is a piece of fabric, with some threads running north and south, and some threads running east and west. When the threads are woven tightly together, the fabric is strong. When the threads come loose in either direction, they blow in the wind.

The threads that run north and south are the things that happen corporately, from the pulpit and the staff, the institution. It's the worship, ministry, programs, the drip campaign, the website. The majority of churches from the Late-Christian era are pretty good at maintaining these threads in the Post-Christian era. The church today still does a pretty good job at being the institution.

The threads that run east and west are where people connect with each other. This is where the fabric is weaker in today's churches. Remember that we form relationships differently now. Let's say that your church is doing everything we've talked about. You have answered all the questions to a visitor's satisfaction. You have communicated with the seventy-five percent of irregular attendees and they're now coming at least once a month.

You're doing everything right, but now, the people need to connect with someone. It's up to the church to offer the opportunity to connect. It is up to the church to think of ways people can show up and participate. If we are thoughtful and a little intentional, we will connect with other people at some level.

One of the best ways for people to connect is to serve together. The church has a universe of volunteer opportunities. There is usually no shortage of serving opportunities; there is usually a shortage of volunteers. There are two simple reason:

1. We ask using passive methods to recruit volunteers.

2. We ask before we connect.

How does your church look for volunteers? Do you put together an annual serving guide illustrating all the fine ministry opportunities available in your church? Do you have everyone fill out an interest survey, promising to share their responses with corresponding ministries? How about sign-up sheets in the lobby or the latest digital registration software? All of these are passive methods in that they do not require one person speaking to another person and asking individuals directly if they would like to volunteer.

Before the Internet and smartphones, the only way to recruit volunteers was person-to-person. As much as I advocate for Post-Christian era

"THERE IS STILL NO SUBSTITUTE FOR PEOPLE ASKING PEOPLE TO VOLUNTEER – ONE PERSON AT A TIME."

solutions, sometimes conventional wisdom is conventional for a reason. It works. There is still no substitute for people asking people to volunteer — *one person at a time* . Unfortunately, in most cases when it comes to recruiting people from the neighborhood and the community, we have to use passive methods to recruit volunteers. That being said, the smaller and shorter the volunteer opportunities, the better passive methods of recruitment work.

What we do not want to do is ask the person who walks through the door for the first time if they'd like to go on a three-week mission trip to the Amazon. Instead, the first connection we want to make with the community is an opportunity to show up *in anonymity and help*. The best is if it's ad hoc, one time, has a short duration, and can be done on a weekend or evening.

For example, you could send the newcomer a text or e-mail with a friendly request. Let's say that the church has a dozen shut-in members and there's been a snowstorm. You could say, "A bunch of us are going to meet at the church Saturday and go shovel some walkways for some people who are not able do it for themselves. Would you like to come?"

Remember we made a promise that if they gave us their information, we'd see what the Holy Spirit might do. We didn't promise that we'd put them to work, but the purpose for inviting them out to a short, one-time event is to give the saints and disciples there the opportunity to start making a connection with the newcomer. The saints who shovel need to know this is their role.

As people are shoveling the walk, they ask about the person whose walk they're shoveling, and then they start talking about themselves. The saint(s) assigned to the same task listens and starts to make connections for the new person. The saints tell the newcomer about other ministries in the church that might meet their interests. As a result, a bond begins to form. After just one hour of snow shoveling, the person who didn't know anyone a week ago has a feeling he or she is now in some way connected and would like to come back to church again. When it is time to volunteer in a bigger way, the saint on the driveway calls the newcomer they met on the sidewalk and asks them to volunteer (in a bigger way) again. This is how the east to west threads are added, one thread at a time, to the fabric that is your church. This is how we begin to close the hole in the bottom of the bucket. This is how the church grows.

At one time, I attended a big church that had three men's softball teams. The A-team was competitive. People had to try out for it and not everyone always got to play in every game. The B-team was less competitive, and most players on it got the opportunity to play a bit. The C-team was the team where everyone played. Generally, the men invited to the C-team were new to the church and were invited for fun. It met the criteria: It was for a short duration, didn't require commitment beyond the first time, and could be done on a weekend or in an evening. Men from the A and B team did the inviting to the C team. The men from the A and B team knew that if enough new people showed up for a C team game, the A and B players would voluntarily sit out of the game.

The interesting thing was that the C-team never stopped producing a harvest. Men were invited to have some fun, but what they didn't know is that there were players positioned, even many from the A-team, who just sat on the bench and let the other guys play because their whole job was to meet the new guys. Many of the new guys who met someone while playing softball eventually met Jesus. Once the connection was made, it was easier to start the evangelism and disciple-making process.

In the Post-Christian digital age, this is how it's done. We need to find things that are off the cuff, short duration, can be done on a weekend or one night, and load it up with saints. The saints need to understand that their purpose is not just to dig out the shut-ins, or play a game, or put together some playground equipment, or get some plants in the ground. These activities are the community's opportunity to connect with the saints and disciples. This is ground zero where we become the church.

We won't get 100 percent of the people to come, connect, or to receive Christ, but it's surprising how many more people we will get to come if we just *personally* ask them. Each person who connects on a deeper level shrinks that hole in the bottom of your bucket. The average church in America has eighty people in weekly worship. All it takes is to connect two families, and that church has just grown by ten percent. It doesn't take much, but it does take being intentional when it comes to connecting disciples and saints with the community and the neighborhood.

DAY 16 PROVIDE CONNECTIONS

Come up with a one-time, short duration volunteer opportunity to offer the church in the next thirty days. Then create a list of newcomers to the church and call them (or have people call them) and ask them personally to participate.

DAY 17

WHERE DO I CONNECT?

Churches are having more trouble recruiting volunteers than ever before. It's interesting that the one place where today's churches have faithfully adopted the digital age is in volunteer recruitment. The church uses all kinds of digital sign-up sheets and volunteer management software. Yet one place where passive digital interaction does not work is volunteer recruitment. Volunteer recruitment is old school all the way. The most effective volunteer recruitment is done person-to-person and one person at a time.

If you ask the overworked volunteers in children's ministry, they may all tell you that people just don't want to help. But think about this. When a person first walks into your church, they enter a place that is obviously run by volunteers. Before they lay eyes on the pastor, they likely see a volunteer parking attendant, volunteer greeter, volunteer usher, volunteer musician, all supported by a volunteer technical team that turns on the mics and lights up the screens. So do we really think that asking them to volunteer is going to come as a surprise? Or that it will be offensive, or met with staunch resistance? I refer to this type of thinking as *"stinkin' thinkin'."* This type of thinking probably has more to do with the people recruiting the volunteers and the methods they are using than it has to do with the potential volunteers' desire to volunteer. Maybe we should consider: *Is there a better way?*

Let's say that you come up with a cool volunteer opportunity that you announce in the worship service. Most people think to themselves, *Wow, that looks like a lot of fun.* To participate, all a person has to do is sign up in the foyer after service. On the Sunday after the cool volunteer opportunity is over when you report the success and how much fun it was, maybe you show a short recap video. How many people who *intended* to participate will say, *Oh no! I forgot!?* Why? Because a person is far more likely to remember the promise they made to *a person* than to remember just to "show up" and sign up at a table on the way out the door. A very important precept to remember is more people truly *intend* to serve than actually remember

"MORE PEOPLE TRULY INTEND TO SERVE THAN ACTUALLY REMEMBER AND SHOW UP."

and show up. Instead of identifying a shortage of volunteers as the volunteer's lack of desire, maybe we should *assume desire* and help them by making registration instant and convenient. Help them schedule the service and remind them a few times so they remember.

Who?

Who is going to do the recruiting? Are you going to ask the person who ended up doing almost everything at an event? We don't want that person recruiting, because:

- That person will call assuming people will *not* help.

- That person will think that if they can't find anyone, they can always do it themselves.

Your best volunteer recruiter is a person who:

- likes talking to people. One church we worked with had a receptionist who couldn't answer the phones fast enough. She couldn't have a conversation that was less than five minutes. The church moved her off the phones and onto volunteer recruitment and the level of volunteerism went through the roof.

- does *not* want to do everything themselves. They like to *talk* about anything and everything, but they don't want to *do* everything.

- believes that people they call are as excited as they are to be a part of this wonderful community, and just need to find a place to plug in.

- works nights and weekends. Volunteer recruitment is a retail prospect with retail hours: that means, nights and weekends.

- doesn't wait until the last minute.

How?

How do we recruit? Let's talk about the series of phone calls. First, a scheduled phone call will always be more effective than a random phone call. Even if you get a hold of someone, ask them if now is a good time; or can you schedule a call in the next few days. Also, sending out recruitment e-mails that are well produced and answer the *"why"* of volunteering for this project and have a *connect button* where a volunteer can schedule a phone call can be very effective.

The first question on a volunteer recruiting call should not be, "Can you come help dig a ditch this Saturday?" It should go more something like this:

"I work with the connection committee, and we want to find a way for you to connect, but we want it to be a meaningful engagement that is fulfilling for you. So, can you give me a minute of your time just to tell me what you like to do?"

You're generally calling someone who was in the middle of something else, so the first call will require a follow-up call. If the person is totally new to your fellowship, you may not know anything about them in advance. You can say: *"What do you like to do either for work or fun?"*

Let's say they respond like this:

Scott: "I work in finance, so I'd never want to do finances outside of work."

Rebekah: "Generally when I do charitable work, I help with finance."

Mike: "All I really like to do is golf, fish, and cook."

Meredith: "I don't know how to do much. I work at Walmart and have three children."

Your second phone call is to say: *"Here are some opportunities coming up in the next sixty days that you might enjoy. Do any of these fit your schedule?"* You might invite the people listed above to:

Scott: Usher one Sunday per month

Rebekah: Count the money in the bookstore on the first and third Sundays

Mike: Serve at the golf tournament, or help cook the meal that is provided at the parenting seminar

Meredith: Greet every other Sunday or serve in the nursery on the first Sunday of each month.

A very important rule to remember in volunteer recruitment is that no volunteer is *ever* turned away. When half the scheduled volunteers show up, you have just enough to get the job done in the allotted time. If fewer show up, you can ask a couple of people if they'll stay an extra hour. When *all* the volunteers show up, you have too many, but you find a meaningful job for *everyone*. You have to respect the time people took to schedule it, get ready, get their families ready, get to the location, and invest the time to serve. After they've done all that, if you turn them away, you may never see them again.

For example, let's say the kitchen fills up with workers. First, your lead volunteer steps back and becomes the instructor and chief chatterer, not the cook, then finds things for people to do. Perhaps normally mashed potatoes are made in a large pot by one volunteer. With multiple helpers, you divide those potatoes into a few smaller pots and put everyone to work. As they work, they'll talk and laugh and *connect*. Who feels more fulfilled at the end of the day: the person who made the whole pot alone, or the people who made it together, or the leader who hung back and just got to know some new people? The answer is, *they all feel fulfilled.*

When recruiting volunteers, remember the purpose. Connecting people to people is why the church must constantly be inventing ways for people to volunteer. Assume desire. The Late Christian-era church looked at volunteering as a way to get things *done*. In the Post-Christian era, volunteering is the way to *connect*. Serving is the best way for people to connect with the life of your church. Connecting people to people is how we shrink the hole in the bottom of the bucket. It is how a church grows.

ACTION STEP
DAY 17 WHERE DO I CONNECT?

Review ten opportunities to volunteer/ participate in the life of your ministry. Then examine the methods used to recruit volunteers/participants. Are they passive or active? Replace passive methods with active methods.

DAY
18

SPREAD THE WORD -
DEVELOP CONTENT

At The Provisum Group, we provide virtual staffing solutions for churches and faith-based charities. We primarily provide services in the area of accounting, finance, treasury, marketing, communication, information services and customer relationship management. One of the toughest challenges we face every day is content acquisition and development for marketing and communication. Essentially, we need our clients to give us some sort of idea as to things like:

1. What is the sermon series?

2. What do you want in the bulletin?

3. What events are being planned?

4. What ministry is happening?

5. How are lives being changed?

Someone has to make those decisions at the client level. And, the decision has to be made soon enough for content to be developed and distributed. You can't finish the bulletin articles at 10:00 p.m. Saturday evening and expect the bulletin to be typeset, proofed, edited, and printed by 8:00 a.m. in time for Sunday service.

So in this chapter, we are going to look at some good guidelines for content development.

Functional is better than cool! I cannot tell you how much time and money I have seen wasted by church staff and leadership over things like colors, fonts, images and graphics. Don't get me wrong. Creativity is important. There is a reason creativity is so expensive. As a left-brained, task-oriented person, I truly appreciate the creative gift. But a B+ creative piece executed well and delivered on time in most cases will produce a much greater return on investment than an A+ creative piece executed poorly and delivered late.

In a church growth class I conduct I illustrate this point by showing the audience of pastors and church workers three different posters advertising food truck festivals (you can watch it at www.connectandgrowyourchurch.com/poster). I ask the group to identify which poster they like best and tell us why. Soon people are advocating (sometimes vigorously) for one poster over the other. Sometimes the debate could go on for an hour if I let it. Then I ask a second question. I tell the group that one of the posters (I don't say which one) will cost $65. One will cost $250. And one will cost $1,200. "Which one do you want now?" I ask. Always the same response. Silence. Then someone whispers, "The $65 poster." Never fails.

Copy Writing In copy writing, less is more. One of the first things I tell my copy writers is "Nobody reads anymore." Now we all know that is not entirely true, but what is true is that video is replacing copy. If a picture is worth a thousand words, a video is worth ten thousand words. We have one client for whom we have to shrink the font and decrease the margins on paper for almost every letter their pastor writes. If you have to shrink the font and shrink the margins to get all the words on the paper, you have too many words. A good rule of thumb is that if you cannot say it in writing in less than 150 words, record a video.

Diversity Matters Sunday morning at 11:00 a.m. has been called the most segregated hour in the United States. The truth is that when people look at your communications, your church, your website on social media, they are looking to see people who look like them. Young, old, single, children, black, white, brown, yellow, men and women, and so on: Make sure you represent as much diversity as you possibly can in all your communications.

Frequency It is far better to tell someone one thing five times than five things one time. Unfortunately, to make this happen, someone is going to be disappointed. The knitting circle and the book club may have to sacrifice one of their communication spots for the parent's day out and the community meal.

Understand the Process Creativity is a process, and so is production, and process takes time. People need time to execute vision. Content is a by-product of the marriage between creativity and production. In the process of creating content there is a back-off schedule. To create a back-off schedule, you start with the date of the event or service you want to tell people about. Then you back up (on the calendar) the day(s) you want people informed about the event or service in question (called "the drop date"). If a piece is going to be mailed, you have to back up about ten days for the U.S. mail. Then you have to back off again for time for the printer to print, the graphic artist to create, the writer to write, the creative team to come up with the concept, and so on. Between each of these efforts you have to allow for time to make edits. All in all, a simple letter can take four to six weeks to properly develop and execute.

Honor the production schedule and expect people to do what they say they will do and be on time. Not only will your results improve but so will your production capacity.

Pay for Experience Whenever possible, hire or engage skilled professionals to create your content and produce it. As we have discussed throughout this book, connection is the tip of the spear of disciple-making and disciple-making is the reason we are here. However, so much of church and ministry communications in the church today are being produced and managed by people who know very little about the science. A worship leader who owns an Apple computer becomes the graphic designer. A youth pastor who made a blog, becomes the webmaster. Having created a blog does not make a person a webmaster any more than owning a wrench makes someone a plumber. However, the same church that will hire and engage a licensed plumber to fix the leaking water heater will engage just about anyone willing to do the job for little or no pay when it comes to creating and producing communication.

"DON'T RELEGATE ONE OF THE MOST IMPORTANT MISSION CRITICAL PROCESSES THE CHURCH HAS TO INEXPERIENCED AMATEURS AND NOVICES."

Don't relegate one of the most important mission critical processes the church has to inexperienced amateurs and novices .

DAY 18 SPREAD THE WORD – DEVELOP CONTENT

Sit down with someone who creates content for your ministry and review some communication content. Review how the content encourages people to come, connect, and grow. Ask the person who produced the content: "How does this content convey our brand story?"

ONLY THE HEARER COMMUNICATES

One of the great truths I have come to learn over the years is that there are many gifted speakers, but few gifted listeners. Do you remember the exercise in elementary school where the kids all sat in a circle, and the teacher whispered something into one child's ear, and then each child took turns whispering what they thought they heard into the next child's ear? It was amazing how much the message changed by the time the last child repeated what they thought they heard.

The truth is that "only the hearer communicates." It does not matter what you think you said. What the hearer heard is what was communicated. If the person doesn't hear you, no communication took place. This is a very important concept to remember in church communication. Very often, people who lead church communication think their job is done once a message is delivered. After all, "We announced it from the pulpit and put it in the bulletin." What about the people who weren't in church? What about the people who are new this week? What about the person who was not listening? What about the person serving in children's ministry? What about the person who forgot? What about the person who doesn't understand the church context?

A great example of context was a church that spent four weeks promoting a study series they called "Understanding Millennialism." They announced it from the pulpit in every service. Sent out e-mails. Made phone calls. Mailed invitations and sent out text notifications. When the day arrived for the first "Understanding Millennialism" class, the church was shocked that over 200 people showed up. The church was even more surprised when they discovered that half the people showed up to talk about their relationships with their 20-35 year old children and the other half showed up to talk about the book of Revelation and Jesus' thousand year reign, often called the millennial age.

Regardless of what we think we have communicated, only the hearer communicates. Couple this truth with "You are not them" and you have a recipe for miscommunication and disconnection. This is why we have to get good at conveying our message in many media to many people. Some people remember what they read. Some people remember what they see. Some people

"REGARDLESS OF WHAT WE THINK WE HAVE COMMUNICATED, ONLY THE HEARER COMMUNICATES."

remember what they hear, and others remember what they do.

Getting people to accurately recall a message is only half the battle. Next we have to get them to behave in a desired manner (for example: give, come, join, help, and so on). In my experience, this is where we really fall short. If you don't take anything else away from this chapter, I hope you begin to understand the difference between an invitation and an advertisement. An invitation tells us "where" and "when" (and maybe "who"). An advertisement tells us "what" and "why": *what* we can expect to experience and *what* we can expect to "get" from the experience, as well as *why* we should care and *why* we will like it.

When it comes to affecting the behaviors of others, *where* and *when* matter to the hearer of the message only after *what* and *why* have been understood and deemed desirable. Take for an example a midweek meal served by a church. What are the *whys* someone will attend? Cheap food? Good food? Lots of food? Or how about no cooking? No dishes? Fed children? A one-hour parent time out? So if the goal is to get more young people to come to your church (for what church is this not the goal in the twenty-first century?) and you think a midweek meal is a good place to start, which of the following communications do you think will work better?

1. At this week's Wednesday night dinner we will be serving chicken and dumplings with homemade bread and apple pie. Dinner will be in the fellowship hall from 4:30 p.m. until 6:30 p.m. and the cost will be $5 per plate with a $20 maximum charge per family.

2. Let us cook and let us do the dishes. Every Wednesday from 4:30 p.m. until 6:30 p.m. in the fellowship hall at ABC Church, parents get a two-hour break! We cook the meal, we do the dishes, and we send your kids home full, tired, and ready for bed. We always have plenty of kid-friendly options and activities. The best part is that the whole family eats for $20 or less.

Which is an advertisement and which is an invitation? Number one accurately describes the event. It gives all the information necessary to show up and eat. Number two makes people want to come (or tries to). *What* and *why* are how we get non-gifted listeners to pay attention and remember.

Finally, we need to remember the concept of few messages and many media. As I shared earlier in the book, if you want your message heard by as many people as possible, you should probably deliver the message many more times than you want to. People are more likely to "hear" (and *remember*) one thing said five times than five things said one time.

ACTION STEP

DAY 19 ONLY THE HEARER COMMUNICATES

Review a recent communication plan with the ministry stakeholder. List all the "whys" and "whats" a person could have in relation to the communication in question. Then change the communication to include the "whys" and "whats" you think are most important to the hearers of the communication.

DAY 20

TELL YOUR BRAND STORY

Get focused and stay focused. Your brand story should be very clear, very simple, and integrated into everything you do. This means that each time you send a message into the community, and especially into the neighborhood, you should ask yourself, "Which part of the brand am I communicating?" To tell your brand story correctly, you will need to develop some tools — words and images — that deliver the brand.

Think about our example of "the great big church with the really nice people who do cool stuff." When that church does something, it cannot use a lackluster image of two middle-aged, overweight workers in an otherwise empty kitchen. It needs to be a full dining hall packed with people, hopefully with someone who looks "really nice" smiling at people eating. Focus means that most pictures of the outside of that church are drone shots with lots of cars in the parking lot. The photographer needs to be directed to shoot building interiors at an angle, so it looks large. Focus on your brand.

Let's say your branding is that you're that church on the corner that says, "We make close connections." Then the images would be the opposite. Small groups, moments of tremendous friendship, and warmth. Lots of smiles. Lots of hugs. Lots of expressions of compassion.

Let's say your brand is a "multi-ethnic, multi-generational church." You cannot settle for pictures of a bunch of green people, a bunch of orange people, or a bunch of purple people. To convey the brand, your primary benchmark pictures need an old person, a young person, and a child, from various ethnicities. That's your *brand*.

Wear your images like you wear your clothes. Each picture, each story is part of the total image you want to convey. It's your responsibility to tell

"EVERY TIME YOU DO MISSIONS, VOLUNTEER WORK, EVENTS, OR THROW A PARTY, SEND A STORYTELLER."

your brand story. It's your responsibility to show people your cool stuff. To do it, develop your tools — your *words and images*.

The Storyteller

Let's say you're putting together a mission team. On the team, you'll assign a leader with the responsibility to get the team through customs, perhaps another one who knows where the team is supposed to go, and maybe another that speaks the language of the place you're visiting. But *it can't end there*. Every time you do missions, volunteer work, events, or throw a party, *send a storyteller*. Preferably, send a storyteller with a video camera. The storyteller needs to be a "brand champion" for your church.

A church we worked with was conducting a typical community clean-up day. The volunteer recruiter had done a good job and had three families on one team that brought their children. Their assignment was to clean up the outside of the home of a shut-in widow who attended the church until her health prevented it. That savvy volunteer recruiter assigned one of the men on the team to be the storyteller.

During the course of the day the team got to know the woman who owned the house and she got to know them. The storyteller asked if she would tell her story on camera and thank the people who helped her. Then he told all the children to gather around her wheelchair as she talked. The result was a short video about everything this church had done for her and how grateful she was. The video ended with a voice-over; and in the background the viewers saw people working, raking, sweeping, and cleaning. They also saw a young child crawl into the woman's lap as the other children took turns hugging her. The day it aired in the church service, there was not a dry eye in the sanctuary by the end of the video.

As a result of one storytelling moment, the congregation saw what their church was doing for the community; at that moment potential volunteers determined to serve at the next opportunity; visitors wanted to hear more about the church; church shoppers felt they'd found their new home; people in the neighborhood that heard about it felt positive about the church, and some wanted to visit; the webmaster was gleeful with a great new video for the home page.

As I stated earlier, the storyteller you choose needs to understand that they are "brand champions" for your church. Storytellers need to understand that their role is to proactively seek out the stories that will illustrate and illuminate your church and its people living out your brand. They need to understand and have a vision for how and what stories positively impact your congregation, community and neighborhood.

I am sure that there were many opportunities to capture stories throughout the clean-up day I mentioned above. But this particular storyteller understood that at one worksite there would be families, children and an older woman who was known and loved by the congregation and this confluence of people and activity were the perfect components for a compelling story of this church living its faith and making people's lives better. This is a perfect example of what you should look for and expect in the storyteller you choose.

Storytelling is a powerful tool for connection and sharing your brand. It's a way that helps people who don't know you, your church or what you're about, be able to connect with you in a positive way. That's the goal of your storytelling – to help people connect with your church and eventually each other for the purpose of making disciples. People relate to stories. They remember them. So find storytellers in your congregation. Get great at telling the stories of your brand.

ACTION STEP

DAY 20 TELL YOUR BRAND STORY

Sit down with someone who is responsible for content in your ministry. Create a plan to capture a story at an upcoming event or happening. Define the desired outcome for people who will hear or see the story. Discuss how to manage the telling of the story to achieve the desired outcome. Get really good at this.

DAY 21

ONE MESSAGE, MANY MEDIA

Precepts determine concepts. If you have the wrong precept, you'll have the wrong concept.

"PRECEPTS DETERMINE CONCEPTS. IF YOU HAVE THE WRONG PRECEPT, YOU'LL HAVE THE WRONG CONCEPT."

A youth leader in a meeting one day challenged me on a decision. We advised the church to mail flyers to remind and invite people to special Easter services that were at a different time than normal weekend services. He pointed out that we had already advertised the service times in the bulletin, on the website, in pulpit announcements, on the church app, by text, by phone, on our social media, and in life groups, so this was just a waste of money, because "no one reads snail mail anymore."

What he couldn't have known is that I'd probably sent a billion pieces of advertising through the mail before he was even born. Calculating return on investment of mailed pieces was not a new concept for me. But I didn't say that. Instead, I helped him understand his precept. The concept he believed was that we were overcommunicating. The precept behind that concept was that "everyone reads every message in every medium." The correct precept is this: the only person who truly communicates is the receiver of the message. You are not them.

Adopting the precept that people are sick of a message is a common mistake made by many church staff members. Especially those people who are responsible for creating and distributing the message(s). The people responsible for communicating the message get sick of saying it. Remember, *you are not them*. The people who are sick of saying the message *are not the same people who are receiving the message*. Just because the church has said a thing *many times* does not mean every one for whom the message is intended has received, read, listened and remembered every (or any) message you sent. This cannot be overstated. When you've been in a church for twenty years, you are tempted to believe that everyone has internalized the rhythm of the church as you have, but that is simply not true.

How many marketers who work for Chick-Fil-A are sick of those cows? But the cows are in Chick-Fil-A advertising because after all these years, they still *work*. The rule of thumb in advertising is that the day you change your campaign is not the day the weary marketers say to change it. The day you change your campaign is when your accounting and database departments say the response is declining and the advertisement no longer generates the desired return.

Chances are, church constituents who are under thirty-five years old get the majority of their information on a smartphone; while constituents between thirty-five and sixty-five generally get their information through e-mails and websites; and those over sixty-five for the most part get their information through a letter or a phone call. The behaviors of these age groups are not as hard and fast as they once were. The days when we said someone had to be young to be digital are gone. Many people I know who are over sixty-five are spending evenings on a tablet looking at videos, e-mails, news, and social media.

Announcements through an app might be the best communications for a college-age student, but it might also be best for retired grandparents who are spending time traveling. Snail mail might be best for a seventy-year-old, but it might also be best for a harried thirty-year-old mother of three who can post the card on the refrigerator and have it front and center on Easter Sunday morning. This is why we make the rule: "one message, many media."

Let's talk about the much-maligned "robocalls" of political campaigns. Although we're living in a digital age, telephone calls still work. Marketers and political action committees don't use robocalls out of nostalgia. They use the telephone *because it works!* Statistics show that older parishioners will likely listen to 100 percent of a robocall message, meaning they'll listen all the way through to the end. When a parishioner of *any* age recognizes a familiar voice on the robocall — let's say, the pastor's — a majority of people who receive the call will listen all the way through. One message, many media.

Let's talk about the much-maligned direct mail that we still see in our mailboxes today. Some people will maintain it doesn't work; but not only does it work, it works even if you solicit the exact same thing to the same mailing list for five letters in a row. There will be diminishing returns with each mailing, so you'll get less money from each letter sent, but the same mail piece mailed five times in a row will keep producing. Why? Because some people didn't read the first four letters. Or if they did, they can't remember what the letter said. *One message, many media.*

In the book, *Minding His Business*, I told a fun story — fun for me, that is. A church did a canned food drive, but refused to try a robocall. I challenged them to conduct the drive their way for three weeks. After three weeks, I'd take just one week and do it my way. On the Saturday before my canned food Sunday, we asked the pastor to record a short robocall that went like this:

"Hi. This is Pastor Smith. Tomorrow is the last Sunday of our canned food drive. I know many of you want to help this great feeding ministry, so why don't you go to you cupboard right now and pull a few cans a food out and put those cans with your Bible or car keys? That way you won't forget. See you in church tomorrow."

Not only did we collect more cans of food that Sunday than the other three Sundays combined, it was the *best attended* Sunday that month! We sent the right message at the right time, through the right medium for the moment. We assumed desire; we assumed busy people wanted to help; we assumed people didn't get the message through enough media, or enough times, to act on it. We recognize that sometimes (many times) people just forget. We became very practical in helping them do what they wanted to do — help other people.

The concept is wrong when the precept is wrong. And when the precept is that you're overcommunicating because staff and communication volunteers are tired or bored of repeating a message, you will probably come up with a wrong concept. It's more effective to say one thing five times, than to say five things one time. Say the same thing through many media. One message, many media.

ACTION STEP

DAY 21 ONE MESSAGE, MANY MEDIA

Review one ministry or event communication plan. Is the message being communicated on the web? Via e-mail? Telephone? Phone app? U.S. mail? Is it being said more than once?

DAY
22

EXECUTE, EXECUTE, EXECUTE

"A brilliant idea accomplishes nothing. Turning that idea into reality is how we put a dent in the universe." Don Corder

One of the biggest mistakes we make in churches is that we treat connecting, communicating, and marketing as a task, not a profession. We

"ONE OF THE BIGGEST MISTAKES WE MAKE IN CHURCHES IS THAT WE TREAT CONNECTING, COMMUNICATING, AND MARKETING AS A TASK, NOT A PROFESSION."

would not give the church's legal responsibilities to someone who once worked at a law office or took a few classes in college. We wouldn't let someone repair the church's electrical system because they once wired a basement. We wouldn't let someone repair the church bus because they know how to change the oil on a lawn mower. All the above would be considered negligent.

But in the church, the responsibility of communicating and connecting with the neighborhood and community is routinely delegated to inexperienced and underqualified volunteers or staff people. Many churches give communications' responsibilities to non-communications personnel. On a church staff, we may give the website to a youth pastor who is good with computers. We ask the secretary to do copywriting. We give graphic arts to the worship leader. Most churches do not have large staffs, so we cannot help but to assign staff members to more than one job, but when we have to give a person two jobs, we need to make one job be their *primary* responsibility. In this twenty-first century Post-Christian era when connecting is king, communications is the *most important* of the two jobs, so it might be better to look for a webmaster who can play the guitar rather than a guitarist who can create a website.

Or we may give communication and connection responsibilities to a volunteer. Churches are organizations run largely by volunteers, so let's consider volunteers for a moment. There are three generations of volunteers — alpha, beta, and gamma. The alpha volunteer usually has passion and competency. We love them. They have carved out their place and execute their job with excellence. And you can't beat the cost of a volunteer. Often, we put them on staff, but sometimes they move on for other reasons. The truth is, no volunteer (or staff person) stays forever. When the alpha volunteer moves on, the beta volunteer moves in. Usually the beta volunteer has either competency or passion, but not both. When that volunteer moves on, the gamma volunteer takes over. Usually this person has neither competency nor passion. This is where communication and connection falls down.

One church we worked with had a volunteer webmaster. A four-year-old boy in that congregation had died of a heart-breaking illness and the church had created a fund in the boy's name. Almost the entire town knew about the boy's illness and death. Many in the neighborhood supported the fund, even though they didn't attend the church. Every year, the church held a major drive for that fund, but on the church's website when a visitor clicked on the children's ministry to check it out, they would see pictures of this boy as a healthy, vibrant toddler. Some volunteer webmaster did not have the competency or the passion (or both) to take the pictures of this poor child off the website after the child died. What message did that send? It said someone didn't care enough to curate the pictures of the church's most famous member.

Our job is to pursue excellence in execution, knowing mistakes *are* made.

- I've seen pastors' names misspelled in church advertisements.

- I've seen the word "Christian" misspelled in newspaper advertisements.

- One church staff wrote a humorous version of a year-end fundraising letter that said the funds raised were for the pastor's new car and lake house. It was an inside joke, but the volunteer who merged and stuffed the envelopes didn't notice there were two versions of the letter. The "joke" letter was sent to hundreds of people asking for a year-end gift.

- A church music director got engaged. Everyone was so happy for her. The church threw an engagement party. Before the wedding, she went to San Antonio with her fiancé for a birthday party. The social media team plastered the trip, the hotel room she shared with her fiancé, all on the church's social media page.

When the church was a leading force in a predominantly Christian culture, marketing, communicating and connecting were secondary activities like the kitchen or the altar guild. These activities were not primary because they were not directly part of the disciple-making process. We did not have to be good at them. But in the twenty-first century, people connect with institutions differently; and to the extent that people initially connect with the church, marketing and communication have become part of the disciple-making process. As such, we need to start treating church communication as the primary function it has become, not the secondary function it once was.

Connection is a process that happens on a continuum. It never ends. We do not get to stop until Jesus comes back. The people in charge of communicating and connecting have to be focused on communicating and connecting, and they have to know what they are doing. One volunteer may have done it right, but the current volunteer may not, and someone over both of them needs to know the difference. We have to continue our good communicating and connecting right through until the end, because that's what we've been called to do: spread the gospel message. Connect with people and make disciples. Execute, execute, execute.

ACTION STEP

DAY 22 EXECUTE, EXECUTE, EXECUTE

Attend a communication production meeting. If your church does not have a communication production meeting, start one and attend.

DAY
23

CHECK THE CHANNELS

No pastor or church leader can be in two places at the same time. No pastor can be home attending the family's needs, making a hospital call, preparing a sermon, and also sit in lengthy meetings about the bulletin and website changes. And yet, there has to be accountability somewhere. Someone has to accept the role of being the Checker-in-Chief, the person who ensures that the message of the church is being accurately and efficiently conveyed. I believe this Checker-in-Chief is sometimes, if not always, the pastor. That means, every now and then, the leader needs to attend the production meeting.

There are two outstanding reasons for a pastor to attend a production meeting, and it is not to know how much construction paper is being ordered for the children's ministry. The first reason to attend is that it shows concern about how the vision is being treated and how it's being produced.

"THE PEOPLE WHO PRODUCE THE VISION NEED TO HAVE A CONNECTION WITH THE PASTOR TO CAPTURE AND EXECUTE THE VISION ACCURATELY."

The vision is valued when the pastor shows he or she values it. The second reason is that the pastor has the vision, but other people produce the vision. The people who produce the vision need to have a connection with the pastor to capture and execute the vision accurately.

One large southwestern church had a very progressive communications team and a visionary pastor that worked in tandem to build a huge congregation with great influence in the community. As the church grew, offices were shuffled. During one move, the communications team director volunteered to move his office downstairs to be closer to his team.

What no one realized was that when the director moved out of earshot and eyesight of the pastor, the entire communications team also shifted and moved. The team was just as great as they had always been, and they read the memos and watched the church calendar, but they no longer had the pulse of what the pastor was really intending. As the message began to drift, the communications team came under criticism. A sharp-eyed consultant was brought in and immediately saw the breakdown in communication. He recommended to the pastor that the team's director be *ordered* back upstairs. Just that fast, everything changed again. The producers of the vision got back on the same page with the visionary.

Most pastors don't have that large of a team, but the point is the same. The pastor needs to know what is happening with those who produce and communicate the vision, and those who produce and communicate the vision need to have a connection with the pastor.

Another large church once deemed they had grown enough that they needed to hire a full-time writer. They had used the services of a writer who moonlighted while working at a corporate job that he hated. He jumped at the opportunity to go full-time with the church, until he learned that he'd have to leave his current church to attend the church where he worked.

The executive pastor helped the writer understand that if he were not in the room, he couldn't capture the pastor's voice. He would not be able to sense the words the pastor used that most moved the congregation. The church didn't need to hire someone to put words into the pastor's mouth. Then the pastor would have to live up to the words the writer wrote. That's backwards. The writer needed to get at the heart of the message. Reading a transcription isn't the same as being in the building. The writer agreed. He was hired. He worked out great.

The people who produce the vision need to share the vision, hear the voice, absorb the passion. For the pastor who attends the production meeting, think "viral." The word *virus* sounds bad if we're talking about health or computers. But the word *viral* sounds good because it connotes a marketing success. Both *virus* and *viral* really mean "infected." Every church team needs to be infected with the pastor's vision.

I encourage pastors to become the Checker-in-Chief, to infect their people with the vision and the passion so both will go viral.

DAY 23 CHECK THE CHANNELS

Review one ministry or event communication plan. Is the plan infected with the brand? The Great Commission? Your vision?

REVIEW RESULTS

The Great Commission is to make disciples of the whole world. That means that the point of the church is to make disciples. And that means, our job in the church doesn't end until everyone is a disciple or Jesus returns, depending on our theology. We *exist* to make disciples of everyone. This means that as leaders, we have to be *on it*. We have to be passionate about what Jesus is passionate about. We have to trust the Holy Spirit to lead us to get the results that Jesus wants, so results should matter.

However, in terms of reviewing results, a disciple made, is a trailing indicator of a process that may have taken years or even decades. If we want to influence the number of disciples being made, we have to control the process that leads to making a disciple. We have to review leading indicators and manage observable behaviors. Let me give you a secular example.

One of my first management jobs was as a field sales manager. My company provided me with an ocean of data on each of the salespeople I led and each of their customers. I was given figures on sales, margin, new customers, lost sales, and back orders. When any of these numbers were not what I (or the company) wanted them to be, I had to figure a way to make the numbers improve. I remembered a top performing salesperson saying to me once: "The more sales calls I make, the luckier I get." I started looking at the call reports of the people I led and I noticed something right off the bat. The best performing salespeople made not only the most calls overall, they also made the most sales calls on businesses that were not yet customers. More sales calls resulted in more sales. More cold calls resulted in more new customers. More new customers resulted in more sales. Sales are not an observable behavior. Sales calls are. Sales are a trailing indicator. Sales calls are a leading indicator.

In the church, we measure things like attendance, giving, baptisms, decisions for Christ and new members. All these are trailing indicators that require a solution when the numbers are not what we want them to be. Many of us are measuring the wrong stuff. For example, when we take attendance, we are measuring the people who showed up. If our weekly attendance is

"MANY OF US ARE MEASURING THE WRONG STUFF."

not where we want it to be, doesn't the solution lie in the people who didn't show up or who have not come yet? Shouldn't we look at who is attending less and how many attended for the first and second time? Doesn't the solution lie in getting more new people through the door and getting existing people to stay and attend more?

If we want more new people to join our church, shouldn't we measure the number of reach events that are on the calendar or the reach of our social media posts? How about the number of door hangers we distributed to the neighborhood last week or the number of new contacts we received this week? Visits to our website? Unsubscribes from our contact lists? Social media likes?

Whatever leading indicators you think are important to growing your ministry, it is important those numbers be brought to you each week. It is important that your ministry has an executive dashboard. The best things about an executive dashboard of leading indicators are fourfold:

1. You get to see the things that are important and move the needle on the trailing indicators.

2. You see the things that need attention soon enough to do something about them.

3. The people you lead know what is important to you and that you are looking at it.

4. When the numbers are current, you know the right people are measuring what is important.

Please don't underestimate the importance of any of these.

Some Leading Indicators

The list below is not exhaustive, but it is a good place to start.

Trailing Indicator	*Leading Indicator*
Attendance	first-time visitors, new contact info collected, lapsed attendees
Giving	first gifts, second gifts, lapsed donors, people giving more, people giving less, first time pledgers, automatic givers.
Disciple-making	volunteers, first-time volunteers, people invited to small groups, first-time small group attendees, people invited to Bible study, first-time Bible study attendees, people in mission, first-time mission servants, new small group leaders, new Bible study leaders.

There are many more things that could be measured, but I hope you get the idea. By measuring the leading indicators and doing it regularly, we can influence the trailing indicators. Over time, you will develop an intuitiveness about those numbers: what is important and what is not. An executive dashboard will become like a road map for you, helping you direct attention and resources to the things that make a difference in the completion of the Great Commission.

DAY 24 REVIEW RESULTS

Review your executive dashboard. Discuss the numbers with people who are responsible for some of the numbers on the report. If you don't have an executive dashboard, start developing one.

NUMBERS MATTER

"Numbers matter because attached to every number in the church is a soul." Don Corder

Working with churches, I've heard some great ideas and a few bad ones. But the most detrimental idea I ever heard, and which I hear more often than I'd like to think, is that "numbers don't matter." The problem with saying that numbers don't matter starts with the fact that we're defining something by saying what it is *not*. In fact, if the Great Commission is our goal, numbers *do* matter because Jesus said to make disciples of "all." If numbers don't matter, wouldn't it be so much easier to work to make our church smaller? If numbers don't matter, then shouldn't we pray for less money?

Think about the logic of the idea that numbers don't matter.

If we're talking about money, and numbers don't matter, then:

- Raising less is better than raising more, and zero in the bank is perfection.

- Not paying our staff should be OK with them.

- We can just try laying hands on our buildings in winter, saying, "Heat thyself."

Numbers matter.

If we're talking about the numbers of *people*, and numbers don't matter, we're saying that *people* don't matter. If we're talking about people and numbers don't matter, then:

- Fewer people coming to church is better.

- It would be OK that some perish without knowing Christ. In fact, the fewer the better.

- We get to determine what percentage of people hearing the gospel in our city is enough for God.

Numbers matter. God is not willing that *any* should perish. When it comes to making disciples, God's number is "all" so our number needs to be "more" not less.

Quick Bible quiz. How many disciples did Jesus have? Twelve. How many people were in the upper room? One hundred and twenty. How many were saved at the Day of Pentecost? Three thousand. How much did the widow put into the offering box? Two mina. How many churches were there? Seven. How many times did God report in His Word, "and their number was…"?

If numbers don't matter, why did God count? And if He didn't want numbers to matter to us, why did He tell us that He counted? And why did He provide us with the totals?

"IF 'QUALITY' IS WHAT WE'RE GOING FOR IN OUR CHURCHES, THEN A BUNCH OF US NEED TO START KICKING PEOPLE OUT BECAUSE, LET'S FACE IT, LOTS OF PEOPLE WHO COME TO CHURCH ARE A MESS."

- Some leaders who say numbers don't matter will claim they have quality, not quantity. But if "quality" is what we're going for in our churches, then a bunch of us need to start kicking people out because, let's face it, lots of people who come to church are a *mess*. Yet they're the very ones we exist to reach, aren't they?

- Some leaders who say numbers don't matter will also say winning doesn't matter. Those are not the kind of people we watch in the Olympics or out on a field of play. If winning doesn't matter, then why does Paul talk about running a race? Why do we call our most important activity "soul-winning"?

- Some leaders who say numbers don't matter criticize pastors who count "nickels and noses." They'll say *that church* or *this pastor* is "all about the numbers." Generally, people who make such an accusation are talking about a church that is bigger than theirs, but what do they say about the church that is smaller than theirs? Do they say that pastor is not *enough* about the numbers? You hardly ever hear anything like that — ever.

It's not a bad thing to measure your results. It's not a bad thing to grow. It's not a bad thing to raise enough money to evangelize the community. The bad thing is if people are *not* coming to Christ. The bad thing is if churches do *not* have enough money to keep their doors open. The bad thing is if disciples are *not* being made. The bad thing is when a church does not reach out to its neighborhood and connect with people. And if a church does not have enough money to reach out to the neighborhood and the community, someone is spending their money on the wrong things.

Churches desire greater numbers because numbers represent *people* and every person has an eternal soul. We attend church *growth* seminars, not shrink-a-church seminars. We'll never see a prayer meeting where the goal is to ask God for fewer and fewer people to come to church, or for less money to do what we're called to do. Numbers do matter.

For people who are passionate about making disciples, we need to be about raising more money for the gospel, and we need to be about reaching and connecting with more people. If our goal is God's goal, numbers matter.

ACTION STEP

DAY 25 NUMBERS MATTER

Ask a ministry leader to present "the numbers" of their ministry. Then review the numbers that matter.

DAY
26

CLICK THE LINK

There is an old saying that says:

You only get one chance to make a first impression.

So why not make it a good one? Where are the majority of your church's first impressions made? The foyer? The greeters? The parking lot? The sanctuary? It was a pretty good bet that one of these was the correct answer

"YOUR WEBSITE IS THE FIRST IMPRESSION THE NEIGHBORHOOD HAS OF YOUR CHURCH."

forty years ago; but today, in this Post-Christian digital age, chances are your website is the first impression the neighborhood has of your church. Websites are the "yellow pages" of the twenty-first century. I can't tell you how many thousands of hours I have watched church folk debate, argue, or advocate on what a church website should look like. I've heard things like: The website is tired. It's too plain. It's too busy. And my favorite: It's "old school."

You have probably had similar experiences in this regard, but how much time have you spent thinking and talking about how the church website is being maintained? There was a time when you could have a website with nothing on it. Today, it needs to have information at the very least. The first place a church leader should look on their website is the calendar. Just for kicks, go to the websites of six churches in your area. You'll find that other than regularly scheduled services and ministries, many church calendars have nothing on them. Sometimes there is little to nothing on the web calendar. When this happens, a church is advertising to the neighborhood that there is nothing going at that church. Perhaps there is zero because nothing is going on. But often there is zero on the calendar only because the communications team is not doing their job. The website is not being maintained.

The more digitally savvy people are, the more they'll think you don't care if links lead to zero or are broken links. Such things declare, "We don't care." Who wants to go to a church where no one cares? I would rather have a tired, plain, old-school website that is well maintained and accurately kept than a cool, hip, and modern website that screams, "Nobody cares."

Imagine that you wanted to buy a car. On the car dealer's website, there's no address, no hours, and no telephone number. Will you go buy a car there? Think about going on a first date. You wanted to look good and be on your best behavior because you knew your date wouldn't assume you're going to get better with time. When you sit down in a restaurant, if no one comes to greet you or help you in the first ten minutes, you know it's usually not going to get better.

The people looking at your church website are looking at it as *consumers*. First they decide to go to church, then they decide which church they'll go to. When someone is on your website and the links don't work, or the dates are wrong, or you have last Christmas's announcements in February, what does it tell people? It says, "NOT THIS CHURCH!" loud and clear.

Back when we were a majority religious force in a predominately Christian culture, we might get away with poor communications and poor web management because everyone felt like they should go to church. But today, we're a minority religious sect in a predominately secular, digital culture. We can't afford to act like a majority religious force or a leading religious force in a predominantly Christian culture. We have to act like a minority religious sect in a predominantly secular digital culture. We have to look like we care and we have to do it digitally. Our first impressions have to show people that we are good at what we do and we care about "you." Poorly maintained websites make bad first impressions. And remember, when it comes to first impressions, you only get one.

Someone in your organization has to care where the links go, and that somebody is probably you. You can't pastor a church, own a company, or be a boss and not care about where your links go or how well maintained the website is. You can preach your heart out every Sunday, build a choir that sounds like angels, lay new carpet, hire a praise team that rocks the house, build a new building, train twenty crack volunteers who give their all for children's ministry, but it's your website that is the first thing to tell the world just how much your church cares.

DAY 26 CLICK THE LINK

Spend ten minutes clicking every link you can on your website and any other electronic communication your church sponsors. Report the broken links or wrong info to those responsible.

DAY 27

CHECK THE PROCESS

You can't pastor a church, own a company, or be a boss and not have some mercy and grace in your heart. People make mistakes, but people are all we have, so we learn how to accommodate the frailties. And yet, at some point, someone in your organization has to care about quality and reputation. Someone has to make sure your church is doing what it says it will do. Someone has to make sure we are working the plan and connecting with people. Someone has to check the process.

In the Late-Christian era, people went to church because "that's what you should do." Today, people walk through the door with a need for which they think the church "should" be able to help. Many are coming because they are at a vulnerable and susceptible place in their lives in which they're probably more ready than they've ever been to accept the gospel message and dedicate their lives to Jesus. We cannot afford to have someone on our team not get the message and the actions of the church right.

One of the first things I do when I start helping a church is get on their website and sign up for communications with a special e-mail account I keep for this purpose. You would be amazed at how many churches have no mechanism for connecting with people on their website. Every so often, I check that e-mail account to see what the church has been communicating. I want to know: Have they been faithful? Are they doing what they need to do? You might be surprised how often I receive nothing or what I do receive reminds me that I am an "outsider." I recommend you do this for your own church, but don't stop there. Get someone to "secret shop" your church for you.

One of the services provided by The Provisum Group is that we send a team to "secret shop" a church. We send groups of people to pose as visitors to test how a church connects with the neighborhood and community. We capture the visit on video and complete an exhaustive report on the experience (Go to www.TheProvisumGroup.com/VisitorAudit to download a copy of the Provisum visitor report). Before we go, I ask the pastor what we will experience when we visit his or her church. Most of the time, we do not experience what the pastor thought we would experience. The way we interpret this is that either the team is not doing what the pastor has instructed them to do, or the pastor does not know what the people are doing. Either way, it's a problem.

One of the things that never cease to amaze me is how hard we have to work to connect with the churches we visit. One of our "must dos" on these visits is we cannot leave until someone writes down our contact

"ONE OF THE THINGS THAT NEVER CEASE TO AMAZE ME IS HOW HARD WE HAVE TO WORK TO CONNECT WITH THE CHURCHES WE VISIT."

information. More times than not, we have to ask an untrained and unsuspecting volunteer if we can leave our contact info and request to be contacted by a staff or clergy member. About a third of the time, we have to walk through the church looking for someone to whom we can make such a request. This is what I call "somebody is having a nice day." They are just not doing their job. And we still wonder why our churches are not growing.

One time, we sent a team to another state to visit the second largest church in a denomination. We had seven people: a couple in their fifties, a young couple in their twenties with two small children, and a single man in his twenties. I had already heard from the pastor what he expected us to experience on our visit. True to form, they had thousands of attendees but still managed to do a wonderful job bringing us in. The facilities were modern. People were friendly and talked to us. The worship was outstanding. Then the pastor stood in the pulpit and told the newcomers that right outside the door, we would find people waiting to connect with us at the "welcome center."

The seven of us had come at different times, through different doors, and sat in different areas. We went out through different doors looking for the welcome center. There was no welcome center. There was a big sign over a small desk that said, "Connection Center." As well-churched people, it was reasonable to assume that "Welcome Center" and "Connection Center" were the same thing. (They were.) What is not reasonable is to assume that newcomers, unchurched and undiscipled people, would know that a welcome center and connection center are the same thing.

As we joined each other one by one, we formed a line in front of a small desk with some dated literature about the church. One of us had a hidden video camera and recorded it. That's how we know that we stood there for thirteen minutes. The reason we stood there for thirteen minutes was that no one was staffing the connection center. Then one of us noticed a small sign instructing us that in the event there was no one to greet us at

the "Welcome Center" to please fill out the visitor "Welcome Survey" and someone would be in contact with us "soon." I immediately noticed two things: 1. There were filled-out surveys from last week still lying on the desk, and 2. The box labeled "Visitor Survey" was empty.

As we stood there, thousands of people poured out of the worship center doors and walked around us to leave the building. No one showed up at the connection center. No one stopped to help us. No one noticed that a volunteer position was not filled at the connection center. The next week, when we reported our experience to the pastor, he was shocked.

Pastor: "How could this happen?"

Me: "I suggest we ask the person who is responsible for outreach and connection."

Pastor: "I'm not sure who that is."

Me: "That's how it happened."

When managing people or process there is one truth I am sure of: You get what you inspect, not what you expect. If you inspect little, expect less. This is one truth every pastor or ministry leader needs to own. Few if any people will care more about your ministry or the people and community you have been called to serve, than you. People need to see you care. They need to see you care enough to follow-up and verify that people are being served and that people are doing what they say they will do.

When people's eternal souls are in the balance, you need to know.

DAY 27 CHECK THE PROCESS

Ask someone to visit your church. Give

them a simple questionnaire to fill out and

have them return it only to you.

DAY
28

ACCOUNTABILITY PAYS

After over thirty years of leading people, I think we can condense management down to four basic responsibilities:

1. Know Your Costs

2. Hire Character

3. Ensure Accountability

4. Stay Out of Harm's Way

My experience with a multitude of churches over decades has shown me without a doubt that the church as a whole is doing a poor job of providing accountability. We are so concerned with how people feel and avoiding a conflict that we have created an environment in which behaviors (or lack thereof) have little to no consequences (costs). I know your church is probably an exception to this rule. Let's make sure.

In the last decades of church life, our old-school thinking was that accountability *costs*. Accountability takes work, diligence, focus, and the discomfort of enforcing consequences for unacceptable behavior and results. Accountability without consequences is inspection. There is no accountability without consequences (positive or negative). Accountability can create anxiety and even conflict especially with underperforming people. We have even confused the absence of conflict with success. In the Post-Christian era, we can no longer afford to think that the cost of accountability is too high. Today, we need to lean into the concept that accountability *pays*.

Where there is no accountability, expectations diminish, and standards fall. If you are in a church without guidelines and consequences, pretty soon the standard will lower so much that any accomplishment at all, no matter

"WHERE THERE IS NO ACCOUNTABILITY, EXPECTATIONS DIMINISH, AND STANDARDS FALL."

how small or trivial, is counted as a "big win." This is usually when we, as an institution, start lying to ourselves.

It is no secret that most American churches are floundering, shrinking, or drying up. As a result of the gospel not being shared, people are turning to false doctrines and false gospels. Sure, the gospel is being shared *in churches*. It's not that preachers have forgotten how to preach or the church has forgotten how to make disciples. The problem is that fewer people every year walk through the door of the church and those who do attend are doing so less and less. The bottom line is that we are not connecting with people.

We once worked with a church that had thousands of people attending every weekend. Every year hundreds of people went into the mission field, hundreds of children went to camp, thousands of people served others. The church was the epicenter of the community it served. Then the church got a new executive pastor. He was actually the volunteer coordinator before being promoted, but he was "real organized." Everybody loved this man and thought he would be a great leader, so he was promoted to executive pastor. Unfortunately he had no management experience and hated conflict. Many on the staff realized that this new executive pastor could be easily swayed and they started to work at making their lives easier.

First came the worship leader who also had website responsibility. He said the existing website was "old school and outdated." We begged the executive pastor not to change the website until they developed a corresponding digital strategy. They changed the entire website anyway with no forethought to strategy or connection. Then there was the youth pastor who said he wanted to engage "fewer youth with better quality" (you can't make this stuff up). Then there was the discipleship pastor who shut down an entire adult Sunday school program with over 300 people participating every Sunday because "only old people go to Sunday school." Or the outreach pastor who canceled three major outreach events per year that used to put thousands of people from the neighborhood on the property every year because "nobody goes to festivals anymore." But all of this and more was not the problem. It was only the symptom.

We advocated vigorously to not take many of these actions. Not because we *thought* they were bad ideas. We *knew* they were bad ideas. We knew it because we had watched church after church make the same decisions and all had ended badly. The real tragedy, the real sin, was that a few months after each of these decisions was made, we showed the executive pastor and the board the impact these decisions were having on the church. We showed them how the new visitors to the website went down by half in the first sixty days after launch. We showed them how new names on the file went down forty percent after they canceled the annual festivals. We showed them how youth attendance went down by seventy percent after the youth pastor changed the program.

Even in the face of all this evidence, the leadership of this church chose to do nothing. Today they get a few hundred for worship. The church is a shadow of what it once was. The evidence we provided was a form of inspection, not accountability. You see, accountability includes consequences (good and bad). All the inspection and measurement in the world is worthless if you do not take appropriate and corrective action, and that includes consequences.

Simply put, accountability means that when people do not do what they say they are going to do, there is a *cost* to the people who are not doing as they promised. Accountability means that when people do not connect,

"IF CONNECTING IS THE TIP OF THE SPEAR OF EVANGELISM, AND IT IS, WE NEED TO RAISE THE STANDARD OF COMMUNICATION, NOT LOWER IT. WE HAVE TO REVIEW RESULTS AND RAISE ACCOUNTABILITY."

there is a *cost*. Accountability pays here on earth and in heaven when our mission is accomplished. If connecting is the tip of the spear of evangelism, *and it is*, we need to *raise* the standard of communication, not lower it. We have to review results and raise accountability.

Let's take a church that convenes on Sunday morning only to find that the pastor forgot to prepare a sermon. We would think, *Oh no! The reason we came was to have a service that included a sermon!* Let's say the following Sunday the pastor forgets again. Or let's say that on four Sundays in a row, the pastor preaches the exact same sermon because of failing to prepare a new one. If this keeps up, how many Sundays would the church continue to convene? Would there be a cost for this type of behavior? Would you take corrective action?

Unlike this example, most pastors *are* preaching their hearts out on Sundays. Many work so hard, they cannot understand why their churches do not grow. The lack of connection is generally not due to a pastor's sermon. The problem is generally that someone else was not executing the connection strategy. They were "having a nice day." Someone didn't get the communications done or did not do them right, and no one held that person accountable. People are not focused on connecting. No measurement is taken, no report given, and no corrective action taken.

The church's job is to proclaim the gospel to a lost and hurting world. When our connection processes are poor, and when the people responsible for those processes are not held accountable, we all pay—the whole church. The cost on earth is shrinking membership, shrinking influence in the culture, and shrinking budgets. The cost in heaven is the loss of souls. Accountability alleviates these costs. *Accountability pays.*

ACTION STEP

DAY 28 ACCOUNTABILITY PAYS

Reward someone publically who has achieved success. Take some form of corrective action privately with the leader of your weakest performing ministry.

CONCLUSION

I hope you enjoyed this book, but more than that, I hope you found this book useful. I hope you found something you can use to grow your church. If you didn't find at least one thing you can use on these pages, send the book back to me and I will give you your money back. This is my guarantee to you. My greatest hope is that you take twenty-eight days and put this book into action. Turn the daily action steps into reality. Treat them like a checklist. Take twenty-eight days and start to connect with the community and neighborhood around you and keep doing it.

It is no secret that the church in the West is in decline and has been for the past forty years. There are certainly exceptions to this rule, but there is no argument that not only do fewer people attend church each week, but faith is falling as a priority in the average life of people in the Western world. Depending on what report you read, less than twenty-five percent of Americans are in church on Sunday. That means over seventy-five percent are not. How did this happen? Volumes have been written on why and how the church finds itself in the state it is in. I will say this: The decline of the

"THE DECLINE OF THE CHURCH TODAY HAS MORE TO DO WITH WHAT WE DID NOT DO OVER THE LAST FORTY YEARS THAN WHAT WE HAVE DONE."

church today has more to do with what we did *not* do over the last forty years than what we have done.

If your church is prospering and growing, if more people hear the gospel in your church and are transformed by it, praise God and pass this book on to a friend or colleague; but if you have been secretly suffering as you watch the church you grew up in, the church you raised your family in or the church you have been called to serve, continue to shrink, put this book into action. If you have been praying for a solution, direction, or idea to reverse decline of the local church you love, maybe this book could be it.

Connection is a process that happens in a continuum. Sunday comes every seven days regardless of how tired or overworked we may be. New people walk through the doors of the church every week and will continue to do so until Jesus comes back; and they all need Jesus. There are always people in the neighborhood around every church who are experiencing some sort of life event that makes them ready to connect with the church right now, if someone will just give them a reason to come. The church can no longer relegate the process of connecting with the community and neighborhood around us to amateurs and novices. Get the right people with the right hearts in place over how your church connects with the neighborhood and community around you. Get proactive about connecting your church with people. Recognize communication and connection as the first step of disciple-making it is.

I hope this book has inspired you. I pray that right now you feel a fresh wind blowing through your ministry and have new vision and direction on how your church connects with people.

The stuff on these pages came from decades of hard work, success, and failure, but the stuff on these pages works! Give it a try.

THE CHECKLIST

Thanks for reading *Connect*. If you read one thing in this book that will make your life in ministry better, then my prayer has been answered. I wrote this book for one reason: Jesus said "all" (people) so the church has to be about "more" (disciples). We grow God's Kingdom on earth by growing the local church. We grow the local church by making "more" disciples. And we make disciples by first connecting with people. But all of this will be for naught if you don't take what you read and turn it into action.

So, if your ministry is going to benefit from what you have learned in this book, then someone is going to have to make sure that things get done. Someone is going to have to bring accountability to the process. To help with that, we have developed a checklist of the 28 action steps described in this book. The check list is designed to be kept in a desk drawer to help you remember what needs to be done today, tomorrow and so on.

To get your free copy of this checklist, go to
www.connectandgrowyourchurch.com/28daychecklist.

You have the plan; a proven plan. You know what to do to grow your church. All that is left is the doing. Go. Connect. Make disciples. Make the world a better place, one person at a time.

Be blessed.

IF YOU'RE A FAN OF THIS BOOK, WILL YOU HELP ME SPREAD THE WORD?

There are several ways you can help me get the word out about the message of this book…

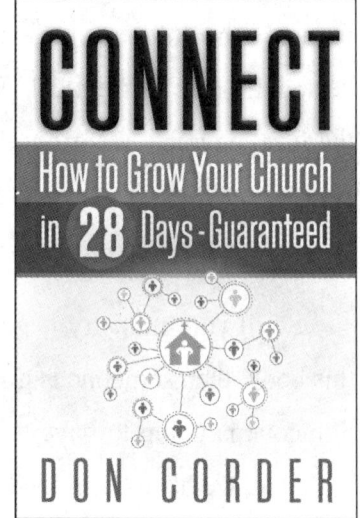

- Post a 5-Star review on Amazon.

- Write about the book on your Facebook, Twitter, Instagram – any social media you regularly use!

- If you blog, consider referencing the book, or publishing an excerpt from the book with a link back to my website. You have my permission to do this as long as you provide proper credit and backlinks.

- Recommend the book to friends – word-of-mouth is still the most effective form of advertising.

- Purchase additional copies to give away as gifts.

To purchase additional copies, book me as a speaker or connect with me for other reasons, go to our website: www.theprovisumgroup.com or email me at: don@theprovisumgroup.com

CHURCH GROWTH IN A BOX

This 6 week guided small group study is designed to inspire your leadership and energize your congregation to grow your church!

In The Box

- A Facilitator's Guide
- Turnkey 90 day plan designed to "jump start" growing your church
- 8 Copies of *Connect-Grow Your Church in 28 Days- GUARANTEED*
- 6 Short video presentations designed to facilitate and jump start each of your small group discussions
- Promotional Tool Kit complete with print ready art designed to invite your congregation to participate in the 6 week small group experience. Kit Includes:
    - Web Banner Ads
    - Customizable Brochures
    - Email Copy
    - Customizable Promotional video

Available in hard copy or downloadable version at:
www.connectandgrowyourchurch.com/InABox

SHARED SERVICES FOR MINISTRY
Spend time on ministry not management.

At The Provisum Group our goal is to help you keep your focus on the things that matter to you and to God. We do this by providing church and not-for-profit ministry leaders with virtual services and remote support in these areas:

ACCOUNTING

- Bookkeeping
- Financial analysis and review
- Treasury Services
- Payroll
- Denominational Reporting

COMMUNICATIONS

- Graphic Design
- Websites
- Bulletin
- Social Media
- Visitor Retention
- Mobile Apps
- Signage
- Event Planning

IT SUPPORT

- Helpdesk Support
- Equipment purchase, set-up and administration
- Hardware
- Software
- Network Solutions
- Mobile, email and database integration

We provide customized solutions to fit your budget whether you are a church or ministry of 50 or 5000. For more information, email us at info@TheProvisumGroup.com or call us at 614-626-2699.

www.TheProvisumGroup.com

THE PROVISUM GROUP
HIS BUSINESS DONE RIGHT